P9-ASB-758

WITHDRAWN

VALUE IN COINS AND MEDALS

VALUE

IN

COINS AND MEDALS

JAMES. A. MACKAY

JOHNSON

LONDON

© James A. Mackay, 1968

XCJ89
.M3

First Published 1968

SBN 85307 013 X

SET IN 11/12 POINT BASKERVILLE AND PRINTED AND MADE IN GREAT
BRITAIN BY MORRISON AND GIBB LTD., LONDON AND EDINBURGH,
FOR JOHNSON PUBLICATIONS LTD., 11/14 STANHOPE MEWS WEST
LONDON, S.W.7

CONTENTS

LIST OF ILLUSTRATIONS

PREFACE

No HOBBY has developed at such an astonishing rate as has numismatics in the past decade. This is partly explained by the better wages and greater leisure time now enjoyed by millions of people all over the world who would have had neither the time nor the money to devote to the hobby a generation ago. It is also accounted for by the rapid growth of all the acquisitive hobbies, whether it be coins or stamps or antiques, as people tend to distrust the value of more traditional forms of investment, and even money itself.

The transition from pounds, shillings and pence to decimal currency has focused a great deal of attention on numismatics in Britain and though many aspiring collectors will be left by the way-side in the scramble for 'key dates' in the obsolescent series, there will doubtless be many others who have taken up numismatics in this fashion and who will gradually turn to the other fields of coins and medals.

The aim of this book is to help the budding collector to spend his money wisely in the formation of his collection, to give the tips and point out the pitfalls. The various aspects of numismatics are examined and something of their investment potential for the newcomer to the hobby is evaluated. Many of the by-ways of numismatics, usually neglected or omitted in all but specialised hand-books, are discussed. An aspect of the hobby which is invariably overlooked, for example, is bank-notes and paper money, interest in which has developed rapidly during the past five years.

I am indebted to my friends in the numismatic trade for their advice and help in the compilation of this book. In particular I should like to express my thanks to Colin Narbeth of the International Banknote Society for much helpful information on the subject of paper money.

Finally, I would like to thank Mrs. Jill Gillot for coping so efficiently with the manuscript and producing the typed version.

JAMES A. MACKAY.

AMERSHAM, BUCKS.
May 1968.

For

ALASTAIR

CHAPTER I

THE STORY OF NUMISMATICS

THERE must be very few people who have not, at some time or another, accumulated a handful of coins—perhaps the dregs of loose change left over from foreign travel, those denominations being too insignificant to exchange at the frontier. These humble coins, relics of last summer's vacation on the Continent, are either left forgotten to gather dust in a drawer, or are handed over to the children to play with. Seldom do they excite further interest. Their more familiar brethren, the shillings and pence, or nickels and dimes (depending on which side of the Atlantic you reside), which are in constant daily use, would seldom be given a second glance as they passed quickly from one hand to another.

And yet is is highly probable that, as long as coins have been in existence, there have been people who have not only spared them that second glance, but who have scrutinised them carefully, taken note of their designs and inscriptions and even laid them aside. Coin hoards are known to exist from the earliest period, hundreds of years before the Christian era, but these would invariably have been amassed for reasons of financial assurance during periods of economic or political instability, and not accumulated for antiquarian motives. Of course, it is possible to be a numismatist, a student of coins and medals, without actually collecting them. Although it will never be possible to say who the first numismatist was, it must be noted that the Greek philosopher and statesman, Pericles (490–429 B.C.) made some intelligent observations on contemporary coinage. Herodotus (484–425 B.C.), in his great *History*, alludes to the fact that coins were invented in Asia Minor.

These scattered references to coins in contemporary accounts perhaps do not add up to much, but certainly by the beginning of the Christian era coins were studied and collected for their own sake. From the *Life of Augustus* by Suetonius, for example, we learn that the Emperor gave 'gifts of gold and silver; again coins of every device, including old pieces of the kings and foreign money' while Pliny the Elder attempted, in his *Natural History*, to give a surprisingly detailed account of the coinage of Rome.

Numismatics, like all other scholarly pursuits, went into eclipse in the Dark Ages. It began to revive, however, in the thirteenth century. The historian Matthew Paris (died 1259) recorded details of contemporary coinage, while Pope Boniface VIII (reigned 1294–1303) is known to have been a serious collector. During the ensuing century the study of coins and medals as a branch of archaeology and the antiquities developed enormously. The late medieval princes and potentates were enthusiastic—though not always discerning—collectors. Because demand exceeded supply, many an engraver or medallist, particularly those domiciled in Florence and Padua, was encouraged to manufacture bogus pieces in the style of Classical Greece and Rome. These 'Paduans', as they are often termed, have often confused relative newcomers to numismatics, but are not without some interest in themselves, tracing as they do a stage in the development of the hobby.

Perhaps 'hobby' is too vulgar a word to use of a pursuit, a science which was followed or studied on a relatively serious level, first of all for the insight which it gave into the social and political history, not to mention the mythology, of ancient times, and secondly, from the Renaissance onwards, for aesthetic reasons. Although the earliest of the great collectors, such as King Alfonso of Naples (who specialised in the coins of Julius Caesar and his successors), were content to collect only Greek and Roman coins, regarding contemporary pieces as barbarisms, by the middle of the fifteenth century the great patrons of art, such as the Medicis, the Sforzas and the Popes, were commissioning the leading sculptors of the period to engrave dies for portrait medals. The medals executed by Pisanello, Gambello and Pastorino in Italy, by Hagenauer in Germany and, at a somewhat later period, by Thomas Simon in England, are lively examples of portraiture in the best traditions of Kimon and Euainetos.

C. C. Chamberlain, in his *Guide to Numismatics*, states that the earliest record of a coin collection in England is in a will dated 1552, that of Edward Beaumont of Oxford. King James VI and I took an intelligent interest in coins and medals and inaugurated a collection for his son, Prince Henry. This collection was enlarged and expanded by his younger brother, King Charles I, after Henry's death; but like the other art collections the royal coin cabinet was confiscated and dispersed by the Roundheads.

Other notable numismatists of the seventeenth century were the Duke of Buckingham, the Earl of Clarendon and John Evelyn. Lloyd R. Laing (writing in *Coins and Medals*, 1965) makes out a good case for the historian and genealogist, William Camden (1551–1623), to be regarded as the 'Father of British Numismatists' since his *Britannia*, first published in 1596, was the earliest work to contain a systematic treatise on British coinage from the ancient British mint of Cunobelin at Colchester down to the time of Queen Elizabeth. Camden's numismatic cabinet was presumably dispersed at the time of his death. His contemporary, Sir Robert Cotton, however, expressed a wish that his valuable library of books, prints, manuscripts and coins be preserved for the benefit of the nation and in fact the Cottonian collections were to form the basis on which the British Museum was founded some 120 years after his death.

To the nucleus of the Cottonian coins and medals was added those assembled by Sir Hans Sloane, who died in January 1753, a bare five months before the Act establishing the British Museum was passed. The eighteenth century was the period of the great collections formed by wealthy gentlemen who were also public benefactors. Such a man was Dr. William Hunter, the celebrated anatomist, whose numismatic cabinet contained some 30,000 coins and medals (12,000 Greek, 12,000 Roman and 6,000 miscellaneous but strong in early English pieces).

The collection was remarkable not only for its extent but for its quality. Dr. Hunter, though he often admitted to having no scientific knowledge of numismatics, was a discerning collector who made good use of the advice of experts . . . 'in all cases where the instinct of the amateur was likely to be at fault'— not a bad procedure to be adopted by the budding numismatist of the present day.

He was a genuine enthusiast who collected coins and medals for the sheer joy of it, but at the same time he seems, at an early stage, to have formulated his plans for the eventual preservation of his collections in a museum. These collections are now, in fact, preserved in the Hunterian Museum at Glasgow University, his *alma mater*. Hunter seems to have had an interest in numismatics from an early age, but it was not till he embarked on his Museum in 1770 that the formation of his cabinet really dates.

A methodical Scotsman, he kept an exact account of his expenditure on coins and medals over the thirteen year period up to his death and it is interesting to note the sums spent on the collection and compare them with its present-day value. Altogether Hunter spent £22,678 18s. 10½d. on his numismatic cabinet; the last purchase was a 'Paduan' gilded medallion (attributed to Alessandro Cesati) for which he paid ten guineas a month before his death in 1783. It would be impossible to hazard a guess as to the current market value of the Hunterian collection, but, taking into account the major varieties which it contains, its probable value would be well in excess of £1 million.

One of the rarest items in Hunter's collection was an Athenian gold didrachm which came to him not by purchase but by gift, from none other than King George III, whose consort, Queen Charlotte, was one of Hunter's patients. The King himself was a numismatist of no mean stature and his cabinet contained two other specimens of this rare coin. This collection, together with the Royal Library, passed to the British Museum after the King's death and greatly enriched the numismatic division which hived off from the Library to form the Department of Coins and Medals in 1861.

A third great numismatic collection in Britain is that housed in the Fitzwilliam Museum in Cambridge. Although the coin cabinet did not become part of the Fitzwilliam till 1856 its nucleus was one of the oldest collections formed in England and is, indeed, one of the oldest collections anywhere in the world to have survived down to the present. This was formed by Dr. Andrew Perne (1519–89), Dean of Ely and Master of Peterhouse.

Dr. Perne entered holy orders in the most turbulent period of English history and successfully changed his views without a qualm, like the celebrated Vicar of Bray, to suit the ecclesiastical mood of the time. The weather-cock on the spire of Peterhouse bears the initials A.P.A.P., which were said to signify 'Andrew Perne, a Papist or a Protestant or a Puritan'—depending on the system then in force. But if Perne was despised for his religious vacillation, he was envied for possessing the finest private library in England. On his death his books were divided between the Peterhouse Library, which he had founded, and the University Library, the latter obtaining also his collection of Greek and Roman coins.

Numismatics developed through the years, from the rather dilettante pursuit of the Renaissance nobility, to the more scientific approach of the scholars of the seventeenth and eighteenth centuries. By the early nineteenth century it was not uncommon for gentlemen to have a coin cabinet as a normal appendage to their library, along with books, manuscripts, prints and drawings. Collectors in the nineteenth century were inspired by the Classical learning on which the Public School education of the middle and upper classes was firmly based. For this reason the bulk of numismatic interest lay in the Greek and Roman series, further re-inforced by the development of the new science of archaeology. The overwhelming predominance of the Classical field in numismatics has lasted down to the present time. A perusal of the periodical publications of the learned numismatic societies bears witness to this, while R. A. G. Carson's *magnum opus* on the Coins of the World, published as recently as 1962, devotes 100 pages to the coins of Greece, and 90 to the Roman series, over 100 to the coins of the medieval world and, by contrast, a mere dozen pages to the modern issues of the British Commonwealth and barely eight to the United States.

Towards the end of the nineteenth century there was a liberalisation in numismatics. In Britain increasing interest was taken in the coinage of the Anglo-Saxon mints and the English and Scottish series down to the end of the preceding century, while on the Continent, numismatists were paying serious attention to Papal coins and medals, the thalers of the German cities and principalities, and their Iberian counterparts the eight-reales of the Spanish and Latin American mints. Interest was still essentially antiquarian, however, and the lifelong numismatist would seldom cast his expert eye on the contemporary pieces in circulation.

The vogue for studying modern coins to any extent probably had its beginnings in the United States. Their relative remoteness from a ready source of supply for classical coins, together with the spirit of insularity or isolationism which pervaded America prior to 1917, combined to turn American numismatists away from the fields pre-occupying their European contemporaries and led them to concentrate on indigenous coinage. This, in turn, because of its comparatively recent nature and restricted limits, has inspired a degree of specialisation which was not to be found in Europe. The coinage of the Colonial period, which began with the New England shilling struck in Massachusetts, dates from the mid-seventeenth century only and pieces in reasonable condition prior to the establishment of the United States Mint in 1792 are generally scarce. For the majority of American collectors numismatics begins with the first cents struck in 1793 and continues through the various Flying Eagles and Indian Head types to the Lincoln cents of the present day. Dimes and half-dimes, quarters, dollars and half-dollars (especially the lengthy commemorative series) are collected avidly, but do not approach the tremendous popularity of the humble cent in all its variations of date, die and mint-mark.

This form of collecting was capable of a much wider appeal than the more orthodox practice of British and European numismatists. The basic material was ready to hand in the form of loose change. This hobby began with a straightforward collection of different dates; for many collectors this rather jejeune pastime was little more than a game, to see how many different dates one could find in the course of normal shopping or business transactions. Gradually, however, this matured with the recognition of different mint-marks and a further development of this form of 'specialization' was that collectors began to observe minute variations in the details of coins from the same date and thus established the existence of more than one die used in the production of the coins. Where more than one die had been used, the existence of several combinations of obverse and reverse dies (known to numismatists as 'mules') was sought. Unconsciously, what had started as a form of collecting despised by numismatists of the old school as somewhat infantile, has progressed into a scientific and technical facet of numismatics.

Of course, the more traditional fields of collecting—Greek, Roman, Anglo-Saxon or medieval European—are not without their technical or scientific adherents but they could never be as numerous, since the quantity of material available for study is relatively small. Nowadays there are two schools of thought in numismatics—the 'scientific' and the 'human'. Whereas the scientific numismatist is well-versed in the techniques of coin production and the rudiments of metallurgy, and has a detailed knowledge of the minutiae of his chosen field, he does not usually have more than a passing interest in the background to the issue of a coin or a nodding acquaintance with the subjects of the coin design and the people, places or events to which they allude.

The scholarly numismatist, on the other hand, is less concerned with technicalities but is more pre-occupied with the coin or medal as a fragment of human history. He will have a reasonable knowledge of the language and dating system used on the coins which interest him, and an ability to see a series of coins as part of the framework of the social, economic and political history of the issuing city or country. Show him a 'Rosa Americana' penny and he will be able to tell you all

about William Wood, who held the patent in 1722–4 to mint
these attractive coins, the circumstances in which they were
struck at Bristol, with a commentary on the political and
eonomic situation in the American Colonies where they werec
circulated.

There are no hard and fast divisions between the two kinds
of numismatist, since inevitably the scholar must learn something of the technical background, while the scientific student
cannot help but pick up at least a smattering of the story
behind the coin. Thus a great many of the collectors who have
come to the hobby through the rather mechanical accumulation
of the dates and mint marks of one particular series are likely
to graduate to a more scholarly approach, at the same time
extending their interests beyond current, indigenous coinage
to the coins and medals of other countries or other periods.

Until four or five years ago numismatics in Britain was the
hobby of a select few who had the cultural and educational
background necessary for an appreciation of the traditional
fields (mainly Greek and Roman) and the money to afford the
pursuit of their chosen subject. An omen of what was coming
was the steady drain of modern material, often of mediocre
condition, across the Atlantic where there was an astonishing
demand for it. Occasional warning notes were sounded in the
numismatic press and it is significant that the editorial in the
first issue of *Coins and Medals* in 1964 dealt at some length with
the threat to the future of the hobby posed by the 'American
Invasion'.

This scramble by collectors in the United States and, to a
lesser extent, Canada to snap up material of all types and grades
was known in Britain and Europe as the American Invasion.
It had two effects: the disappearance of a great deal of coins
and a consequent increase in prices. A secondary effect was to
heighten interest in numismatics in Britain, aided and abetted
by more frequent reports concerning the hobby in the lay press.
Collecting on American lines, i.e. essentially modern coins
according to dates and mint marks, spread rapidly in Britain
and enormously accelerated the growth of the hobby. Some idea
of its development can be obtained from the figures of clubs

PLATE I

BRITISH COINS

(1–2) George III halfpenny and penny; (3) Victoria copper halfpenny; (4–5) Maundy 1d. and 2d.; (6–8) Victoria 3d., 4d., 6d.; (9–11) George V florin, half-crown and shilling; (12) Obverse of decimal coins; (13–14) New 10d. and 5d.

and their membership. In 1963 there were thirty clubs and societies in existence in the United Kingdom, ranging in size and antiquity from the Royal Numismatic Society (founded in 1836) with a membership of 650, to the Horncastle and District Coin Club, founded that year with a membership of 30.

In 1964 four new societies were founded (Birmingham, Derbyshire, Leicestershire and Reading) and another six the following year (Anglo-American, Aberdeen, Devon, Loughborough, Scunthorpe and Winchester) In 1966 there were nine new societies and more than 20 in 1967. Numerically speaking, Britain still lags far behind the United States, which has more than 2,700 clubs and an estimated 8,000,000 collectors in a population of 200 millions. On this basis Britain should have 2,000,000 numismatists (or, at least, people showing more than a modicum of interest in coins). The total membership of numismatic societies amounts to about 2,500, of which slightly under half consists of the membership of the Royal Numismatic Society (650) and the British Numismatic Society (400). If it is assumed that a good proportion of the members of the two national societies are also members of local societies then the true number of active numismatists is probably about 2,000. Between this conservative estimate, and the potential figure a thousand times larger, lies the real number of collectors, many of whom are content to plough a lonely furrow without joining a club.

The lone wolves, however, are a force to be reckoned with, as can be seen by the increase in coin-dealing and the sales of numismatic publications in the past four years. Before 1964 there were no more than half a dozen large coin dealers in the United Kingdom, with a fair number of businesses which dealt in coins and medals as a side-line. The 1968 *Coins and Medals Annual* listed 90 dealers in this country, an enormous increase in four years. This mushroom growth might not have been entirely beneficial to the hobby, since it must inevitably have attracted some persons to engage in dealing with neither the necessary expertise or capital, but in 1966 the established dealers recognised that they had to band together to protect their profession from unethical practices and, to this end, the Professional

Numismatists' Association was founded '. . . for the purpose of maintaining a high professional standard and safe-guarding the numismatic market in Britain.'

Already most of the reputable dealers have joined the P.N.A. and it is well on the road to enjoying the reputation which has already been accorded to the Philatelic Traders' Society, the comparable body in the world of stamps.

Until 1964 numismatic publishing in the United Kingdom was a hazardous business and scarcely to be regarded on a commercial scale. Apart from a brief period in the 1890s when C. Hearn Nunn published a number of ephemeral periodicals dealing with numismatic topics, no magazine of a purely commercial nature devoted to the hobby appeared till 1964 when Link House Publications (which had previously run a numismatic column in *The Stamp Magazine*) brought out *Coins and Medals* as a quarterly.

Prior to that date the only periodicals catering to the numismatist in Britain were either the house journals of the leading dealers or the bulletins of the great national societies. There existed no magazine of a more general nature, to entice the layman into the hobby and develop the interest of the beginner or general collector. Now there are several excellent periodicals, not to mention annuals, which have the beginner and medium numismatist in mind, and it has been estimated that their combined circulation is somewhere in the region of 50,000–60,000 copies of each issue—a sure testimonial to a vast awareness of numismatics in general. The range of numismatic literature, which is dealt with more fully in Chapter V, is exceedingly diverse nowadays and there are few branches of the hobby which are not now well documented with excellent hand-books and catalogues.

Numismatics—or, perhaps, its humbler brother, 'coin-collecting'—has trebled in popularity in Britain in the past four years. The situation was not as desperate as it was in the United States where the mass craze for coins has caused periodic shortages of certain denominations and forced the U.S. Treasury to mint coins dated 1965 after that year had ended, in order to defeat speculation. There was even some attempt to introduce legislation to make illegal the sale of United States coins above their face value. Nevertheless the rumours in Britain last year that no halfpennies were to be minted after 1967, on account of impending decimalisation, caused something of a 'run' on this humble coin. There was some brisk trading in sealed £5 bags of halfpennies, in uncirculated condition straight from the Mint, as 'an investment,' though the futility of hoarding a coin of such low basic value in quantities of 2,400 should have been obvious to all concerned. The Mint very neatly put an end to speculation of this sort by announcing that not only was the production of halfpennies still in progress but that, from then onward, any future minting would be dated 1967.

CHAPTER II

WHAT MAKES A COIN VALUABLE?

IT IS A FACT—sad, perhaps, but true—that the 'profit motive' looms very large these days in all the acquisitive hobbies and numismatics is no exception. Although true scholars and antiquarians affect to ignore the more sordid aspects of the hobby it has to be admitted that, in this hard, materialistic age, the financial aspects of coin and medal collecting are of great interest to the bulk of its devotees. Consequently, and especially with the newcomer in mind, this chapter is written in the hope that it will explain in some measure the factors which add up to govern the actual value and investment potential of a coin. Basically there are seven criteria which can be applied to every coin in an attempt to assess its future prospects. These factors are design, metallic content, numbers issued, theme, country of issue, the prevailing political and economic situation, and last—but by no means least—condition.

DESIGN

Generally speaking, the maxim 'a thing of beauty is a joy for ever' applies to coins as to anything else which has any pretensions to being an art-form. For this reason a great deal of time, trouble and money is expended nowadays by governments in selecting competent artists and designs which are aesthetically appealing, even for the most mundane coppers.

Thus, in Britain, where decimalisation is not due to take place till 1971, the Royal Mint Advisory Committee in 1966 invited artists of established reputation in coin and medal work to submit drawings for the reverse designs of the decimal coins. The Advisory Committee also welcomed sketches from any

artists, including those domiciled in other parts of the Commonwealth, who had not yet done work for the Mint but who would
be able, if asked, to execute plaster models. The Advisory
Committee began examining the designs submitted in January
1967 and by the end of that year had made a careful selection.
By the time this book is published (late 1968) the plaster models
will have been sculpted, the dies engraved, and the first of the
actual coins put into circulation.

The present process, spread over a period of several years, is
probably the most revolutionary one ever to have involved the
Royal Mint, surpassing even the great Recoinage of 1816–17.
The inscription 'New Penny' or 'New Pence' and the prominent
inclusion of numerals ($\frac{1}{2}$, 1, 2, 5, 10, 20) in the designs have
resulted in a radical departure from the more traditional
designs of the obsolescent series. It is interesting to note the
conservatism which has marked British coins since the Restoration in 1660—the recurring motifs of Britannia in all her
variations and the different interpretations of the heraldic
emblems and flowers of the United Kingdom. Now, however,
Britannia has been dismissed, to make way for the crowns,
lions and portcullis of Mr. Ironside whose designs have been
adopted.

Innovations have been comparatively few, but these stand
out as landmarks in the development of coin design. They
range from Pistrucci's magnificent St. George (said to have
been modelled on a waiter from Brunet's Hotel in Leicester
Square) to the delightful little Robin on the now vanished
farthing. The halfpenny and brass threepence also introduced
in 1937, with their respective motifs of the *Golden Hind* and
Thrift flowers, marked a welcome change towards greater
pictorialism, while the crowns of the present reign, particularly
those depicting the Queen on horseback and portraying Sir
Winston Churchill, have caught the public eye. Another
design which has always had great appeal for British numismatists is the 'standing Britannia' which graced the reverse
of the Edwardian florins. Though certain dates are theoretically
more plentiful than their Victorian and Georgian predecessors
and successors they are regarded more highly—and therefore

command a far higher market value. The following table of
florins for the last decade of Queen Victoria ('Veiled Head'),
the reign of Edward VII and the first decade of King George V
gives an accurate picture of the relative market values of
florins of different years, in various conditions (the abbreviations are explained later in this chapter). The table is based on
the prices estimated in the admirable survey serialised in *Coins
and Medals* (1967). I have added the figures of coins minted
for comparison.

Year	Mintage	Fine	VF	EF	Unc.		B. Unc.		
1893	1,666,103	25/-	45/-	£6	£7		£8	10	0
1894	1,952,842	£1	£3	£6	£7	10 0	£9		
1895	2,182,968	£1	£3	£6	£7	10 0	£9		
1896	2,944,416	£1	£3	£6	£7	10 0	£9		
1897	1,699,921	25/-	65/-	£7	£8		£9	10 0	
1898	3,061,343	£1	£3	£6	£7	10 0	£9		
1899	3,966,953	£1	£3	£6	£7	10 0	£9		
1900	5,528,630	£1	£3	£5	£6		£8		
1901	2,648,870	£1	£3	£5	£6		£8		

Edward VII

Year	Mintage	Fine	VF	EF	Unc.	B. Unc.
1902	2,189,575	30/-	£4	£9	£11	£13
1903	1,995,298	45/-	£6	£12	£15	£18
1904	2,769,932	45/-	£6	£12	£15	£18
1905	1,187,596	£3	£8	£22	£30	£40
1906	6,910,128	30/-	£4	£10	£12	£14
1907	5,947,895	30/-	£4	£10	£12	£14
1908	3,280,010	£3	£5	£11	£13	£15
1909	3,482,829	£2	£5	£11	£13	£15
1910	5,650,713	35/-	90/-	£10	£12	£14

George V

Year	Mintage	Fine	VF	EF	Unc.	B. Unc.		
1911	5,951,284	6/-	15/-	£2	50/-	£3	15	0
1912	8,571,731	5/-	14/-	35/-	48/-	£3		
1913	4,545,278	7/6	17/6	45/-	£3	£4		
1914	21,252,701	4/-	12/6	30/-	£2	50/-		
1915	12,367,939	4/-	12/6	30/-	£2	50/-		

Year	Mintage	Fine	VF	EF	Unc.	B. Unc.
1916	21,064,337	4/-	12/6	30/-	£2	50/-
1917	11,181,617	5/-	15/-	35/-	45/-	55/-
1918	29,211,792	4/-	12/6	30/-	£2	50/-
1919	9,469,292	5/-	15/-	35/-	45/-	55/-
1920	15,387,833	3/-	10/-	32/6	£2	50/-

It will be seen that, for example, roughly comparable quantities of florins were minted in 1900, 1910 and 1911 yet, in Brilliant Uncirculated condition, the Edwardian coin rates almost twice as much as the Victorian and four times the Georgian. At the other end of the scale, in Fine condition, the Edwardian coin is worth half as much again as the Victorian and almost six times the Georgian, so it must be assumed that, if the quantities available in each grade are parallel, the Edwardian florin must be worth more because it is in greater demand and it must be inferred that its outstanding design has something at least to do with it.

The range of coins of the world is too vast for all but the most general of statements with regard to design. Undoubtedly the popularity of Greek coinage from the period between the end of the Persian Wars and the accession of Alexander the Great (480–336 B.C.) stems largely from the technical virtuosity of the designers, with their increased delicacy in the treatment of details and greater freedom of movement in the modelling of the human figure. The introduction of portraits of the living Emperor, which characterised the Roman Imperial coinage, marked a great development in historical portraiture and accounts for much of the interest shown in these coins. Perennially in favour are the large thalers struck by German mints in the sixteenth and seventeenth centuries, often imaginative and always vigorous in execution. We may see something of their spirit and lively design in many of the modern crown-sized commemorative pieces and the lengthy series of commemorative half-dollars minted in the United States between 1892 and 1954.

METALLIC CONTENT

At some time or other coins have been minted in almost

every metal known to mankind. The actual metal used, however, only begins to assume financial importance when all other factors are equal. At one extreme are the two unstable metals, tin and lead, which, though cheap, have never been popular on account of their softness and embarrassing lack of durability. Tin in particular is notorious for its propensity to change its density at different temperatures. 'White tin' becomes unstable below 18°C and is swiftly transformed into the lighter, bulkier 'grey tin' which finally disintegrates into a fine greyish powder. This unfortunate transformation tends to spread like an infection from one piece to another and poses special problems for the collector in preserving them. Coins made of tin have been struck on very few occasions. In order to relieve a depression in the Cornish tin-mining industry in the 1680s, when the market value of the metal slumped disastrously, farthings were minted in 1684 under King Charles II, and farthings and halfpence in the reigns of James II, and William and Mary. The coins were very unpopular and were easily forged; consequently their release was terminated in 1692 and the manufacturers who held the contract to produce copper coins the following year were obliged to accept up to £200 a week in tin money in exchange.

The stability of these coins was further reduced by the presence of a copper plug in the centre, supposedly as a precaution against forgery, but which actually seemed to increase the electro-chemical corrosion of the coins. Although these coins have been shunned by the great majority of numismatists the very few which have survived in collectable condition are now excessively rare and consequently command high prices, out of all proportion to their intrinsic value.

Lead is an unattractive metal, soft, dull and with a tendency to oxidise unpleasantly. For the latter reason especially, relatively few examples of coins in this material have survived and these also are therefore rather expensive. Lead seems to have been fairly popular in the Orient. As long ago as the third century B.C. the Ardhras of southern India were striking coins in lead, while, in the later periods, Japan, the Dutch colonies of Ceylon and Java, the Portuguese settlements in

India, and mid-nineteenth century Siam produced lead coins. In classical times lead was used in Bactria, Egypt, Numidia and even in Gaul, but such pieces are very rare nowadays.

Pewter, an alloy of tin and lead, is more durable than either of its components. In spite of its cheapness, however, it has seldom been used for coinage and then only in emergencies when precious metals were not available to the same degree. Consequently the few pewter coins extant are highly sought after and extremely valuable. Halfpence, pennies and crowns were struck by King James II in 1690 during the so-called Williamite War in Ireland.

Most low-denomination coins, from earliest times to the present day, have been struck in copper or one of its alloys. The term 'coppers' is, in fact, still used colloquially to denote pennies and halfpence although these coins ceased to be minted in copper in 1860. The best-known copper alloy is bronze (a mixture of copper and tin with a small percentage of zinc) which has been used since biblical times. Less ancient is brass, which the Romans compounded of four parts copper to one of zinc, and which has been used increasingly in modern times as a substitute for precious metals. The expression 'not worth a brass farthing' which dates back to the early sixteenth century, symbolises the contempt with which this metal has usually been held (though, conversely, the word 'brass' has been used in England for centuries as a synonym for money). Though bronze and brass are cheap metals it should be noted that the most valuable modern British coins are the 1933 penny (bronze) and the Edward VIII threepence (brass). Of the former, only seven are believed to have been struck, mainly for inclusion in sets buried under foundation stones, but examples have been preserved in the Royal Mint Museum and the British Museum. Only one specimen got into private hands and this was apparently sold by Spink and Son recently. The Edward VIII threepences were produced in 1936, but not released on account of the king's abdication. A few specimens got into circulation, however, and have recently been sold for prices between £500 and £1,000.

Aluminium, as a coinage metal, made its debut in 1907

when it was introduced for the cents and half-cents of British East Africa (Kenya and Uganda). It was regarded as unsatisfactory and replaced in 1909 by cupro-nickel which was almost as cheap, but more 'substantial'. The aluminium coins of British East Africa, on account of their relative scarcity, are now quite highly priced compared with their cupro-nickel replacements. Aluminium coins were minted during the First World War in Germany—one of the earliest countries to adopt 'ersatz' materials for coinage—and again, during and after the Second World War. Many countries, indeed, finally dispensed with the need to strike their coins in metals possessing an intrinsic value and have continued to use aluminium to this day. The German Democratic Republic has used aluminium for all its normal, everyday coinage, from 1 pfennig to 2 marks, issued during the past twenty years; these coins are as light in one's pockets as they are in the estimation of the financial world. In countries such as Czechoslovakia, Greece and Japan, aluminium is reserved for the lowest denominations only.

Germany was probably the earliest country to use pure zinc in the manufacture of coins, the first issue being in denominations from 5 to 50 centimes for use in the occupied districts of Belgium and 5, 10 and 25 centimes coins for use in Luxembourg in 1915. The use of zinc coins extended to the Fatherland in 1917 (10 pfennigs) and was retained for this denomination till 1922. Zinc coins were circulated in many European countries under German occupation during the Second World War, while the United States adopted zinc-coated steel for the Lincoln cent minted as a temporary measure in 1943. While most of the zinc coins of the world are held in as little esteem as their aluminium counterparts it should be noted that the Lincoln cent mentioned above is rated at twelve times the value of the normal bronze issue.

Two other metals used by Germany before and during the First World War for coinage were iron and nickel. While iron is one of the least attractive metals for this purpose, pure nickel has a most pleasing appearance, not unlike silver. Italy produced some attractive nickel coins before the Second World War, while Canada, appropriately, struck a 5 cents coin in nickel in 1951 to commemorate the bicentenary of the isolation of this metal.

Nickel alloyed with other metals, particularly copper, has been known since the third century B.C. when it appeared in the coinage of Bactria. The United States was among the first of modern countries, however, to adopt cupro-nickel for its coinage, the 1 cent 'Flying Eagle' type of 1856–8 and the first issues of the 'Indian Head' cents (1859–64) being among the best known examples. More than a century has now elapsed since the first of the 'nickels'—5 cent pieces—appeared in 1866. Britain substituted cupro-nickel for silver coins in 1947, but this debasement of the metallic content did not in itself affect the value of the coins. In fact the sixpences of 1947, for example, are more highly regarded than their silver predecessors of 1946 since a far smaller quantity were minted than usual.

There have been several other interesting experiments in coinage metals—stainless steel (acmonital) used by Italy, steel-coated with bronze or brass for the low denominations of West Germany, and the unusual tombac-brass 5 cents of Canada (1942–3). With the exception of the latter, however, (which is in great demand for curiosity reasons as much as anything) few of these coins are valued on account of their metallic content.

One would expect quite a wide gulf between the base and the precious metals in their respective effects on the value of a coin. With silver, at any rate, the intrinsic value of the coin only begins to assume importance when the coin deteriorates in condition below that grade normally collected. For this reason even poor quality, worn specimens of pre-1920 British coins are now worth more than twice their face value. For many years now people have been hoarding away the few examples in circulation, which have not been called in by the Royal Mint for melting down. By comparison, however, uncirculated specimens of even the common dates of the cupro-nickel series have a value to collectors far in excess of their face value.

Gold has been treasured by mankind since the earliest times and since the seventh century B.C. it (or its silver alloy, electrum) has been turned into coin. In the form of coins, gold has always been a convenient means of investing one's wealth and only present legislation (which, because of its importance, is the subject of a separate chapter) has prevented gold-hoarding from assuming alarming proportions.

During 1967 the value of silver increased sharply, aided by the 14.3 devaluation of sterling in November. By the end of the year the price of silver had risen to 18s. the Troy ounce, which meant that the .500 fine silver half-crowns minted between 1920 and 1947, containing about a fifth of an ounce each, were now worth 3s. 7d. So it is to be expected that these and the lesser denominations (which contain a proportionate amount of silver) will rapidly disappear as the banks return them to the Mint for melting down or those people fortunate to find them in their change hold on to them. It is unlikely, however, that hoarders of worn silver coins will ever be able to profit by this practice, since, apart from the large quantities required to make it worthwhile, there are severe strictures against the melting down of coins. Under the Gold and Silver Export Control Act of 1920 melting down coins is an offence punishable by a £100 fine or two years' imprisonment, or both.

NUMBERS ISSUED

The law of supply and demand is one which has the greatest influence in determining the value of a coin, as is the case with most other forms of collectable material. If only a few specimens of a particular coin are in existence it will obviously be worth a great deal more than another coin, available in far greater quantities, provided of course that the demand is comparable.

Where the exact numbers of coins in existence are known, collectors and dealers alike have a positive guide to relative values. Figures are available for the mintages of British coins since the early years of the nineteenth century, for example, and this enables numismatists to form an idea of a coin's probable value by comparison with other dates (see the table of florins given on page 24). Of course, the figure minted does not necessarily give a proportionate idea of a coin's true scarcity since it can never be known what percentage is in uncirculated condition and what percentage is in lesser grades.

Other 'imponderables' which may affect the scarcity (and hence the value) of a coin are factors such as the last year of a reign or a series and minting for use abroad. Thus the former factor may serve to focus the attention of collectors on a coin while it is still current, causing a larger proportion of the mintage to be laid aside in collectable condition than usual. Farthings, for example, tend to have survived in better grades than halfpennies and pennies which always had a wider circulation. In the latter factor cited above one finds that in certain years (e.g. 1951) pennies were minted, not for home consumption, but for use in colonial territories which use sterling. Thus of the 120,000 minted that year, few would have found their way back to the United Kingdom in the highest grade of collectability—unless they were deliberately repatriated by coin dealers. In this instance a comparatively low mintage figure has to be judged in conjunction with the fact of overseas circulation to arrive at the true scarcity of the coin.

In the matter of coins available in collectable condition the student of classical series is faced with some problems. He does not possess exact figures of mintages, even if these could have any bearing on the numbers of coins that have survived. Only in the extreme case where a coin is either unique, or so excessively rare that the few recorded examples are all accounted for, can a reasonably exact attempt be made at a market valuation. Even here, there are pitfalls. The sudden discovery of a hoard may bring to light hitherto scarce items in large quantities and although it is the case nowadays that the best of such material is creamed off into museum collections, a great deal of it inevitably comes on to the market and is bound to have a downward effect on values.

THEME

Although numismatics, particularly the classical branch, is to some extent concerned with the subject of the design of a coin or a medal (cf. Anson's great *Historia Nummorum* which is arranged according to the themes of the coins as a guide to identification), coin collectors have not as yet become obsessed by the subjects depicted in the manner that their philatelic confrères have. Yet there are subtle indications that thematic collecting has already arrived and may gain enormously in popularity. As usual, the Americans appear to have taken the lead in this form of collecting. There are many collectors who confine their activities to pieces depicting mythology or heraldic devices or horses, for example, while the recent publication of a book entitled *Numismatic Fish and Ships* (dealing with coins having a maritime flavour) shows the extent to which thematic collecting has gone already.

The popularity of certain themes was probably seen most clearly in recent years in the proliferation of medals commemorating the late Sir Winston Churchill and President Kennedy. This even went as far as the Yemen and Sharjah issuing 'crown' pieces portraying the respective statesmen. Perhaps it is not out of place to mention that both these Arab states were remarkably quick off their mark in producing postage stamps in honour of Churchill and Kennedy.

Whether collecting on thematic lines will ever affect numismatics to the extent that it has philately is doubtful, but it seems certain that the increase in the number of commemorative coins in recent years has made collectors more conscious of the subject matter depicted on them.

COUNTRY OF ISSUE

The country of origin of a coin is generally immaterial where items of the classical or medieval periods are concerned, but this is a factor which has some bearing on modern pieces since much of the demand for them is stimulated by indigenous collectors. Thus the modern coins of Britain, Canada, the United States, France, Italy and Germany are keenly sought after by numismatists resident in these countries. Whereas an academic interest is shown in the coinage of, say, Bulgaria, there is unlikely to be the same investment potential that a collection of British coins since 1816 would have, since the indigenous numismatic activity in Bulgaria is on a scale much smaller than in Britain. A shrewd numismatist, however, might consider the coins of a currently unpopular field, in which he would not meet with much competition and in which prices would be correspondingly reasonable. There is always the possibility that what is unpopular to-day may become fashionable to-morrow.

Current coins are, not surprisingly, cheapest in the country of issue since one can usually pick up items in collectable condition in the course of normal business. In order to obtain coins in uncirculated condition, however, it is usually necessary to purchase them from a dealer, but here again they should be more plentiful, and therefore cheaper, in the country of origin.

If that country has a strong internal numismatic following, the demand for these coins will be high in the country itself so it will not be possible to look for bargains there. The converse is also true. I remember, as a schoolboy, purchasing a parcel of Dutch coins from a dealer in Glasgow 'for a song' and taking them abroad with the intention of spending them in the Netherlands. Four of the coins were half guilders which had been demonetised many years earlier. Finding that I could not spend them I took them to a dealer in The Hague who was delighted to pay me six guilders for them. Not so long ago I found a current 5-franc piece and several 1-franc pieces in a dish of coins in Oswestry Market marked at fourpence each—but colossal ignorance of this sort is extremely rare and usually operates in reverse, with general dealers in the 'antique' trade tending to overprice their coins in order to ensure that nothing of real value escapes them unconsidered.

POLITICAL AND ECONOMIC SITUATION

Throughout history the unsettled political and economic situation of a country has always been reflected in people's tendency to hoard 'good' coins—silver and gold. In the present world situation speculators are generally unable to take advantage of precious metal coinage in circulation since few countries nowadays have other than a token coinage (i.e. whose face value bears no relation to intrinsic value).

In those countries where it is possible to purchase gold, either in coin or in bullion, there are a great many people who avail themselves of the opportunity to do so, even though they thus forgo the chance of earning interest on their capital. The

Fränkischer Tag of Bamberg, for example, recorded in 1958 that the West German banks sold about 500 million DM of gold coins to the public in the previous year. Buyers of 20 mark pieces had to pay DM 5.25 per gram fine gold content which, though expensive, was surprisingly cheaper than purchasing gold in bullion (ten-gram bars cost DM 57), while Austrian 100 kronen pieces worked out more cheaply at DM 5.14 per gram.

In the unsettled economic situation prevailing in Britain, since 1964 there was a marked increase in gold hoarding, the effects of which are dealt with more fully in Chapter III. Now that legislation has killed gold hoarding in Britain speculators are undoubtedly turning to other coins, thereby forcing prices up unrealistically. This is seen at its most acute in certain modern limited series, proof sets and commemorative pieces, though it is unlikely to have a serious effect on the classical series or coins whose true numismatic interest far outweighs their attraction to the 'collector' with only a superficial knowledge of the hobby.

CONDITION

All the other factors affecting the value of a coin fade into relative insignificance beside the condition factor. Of course, in cases where coins are either unique or very rare, numismatists have to be satisfied with grades of condition which, in commoner pieces, would be quite unacceptable. At the other extreme, modern coins which are still in circulation should not be collected unless they are in almost perfect condition.

The word 'almost' is unfortunately significant since the modern techniques of coin production are such that one very seldom finds a piece which does not bear some blemish on it. The highly mechanised processes employed nowadays mean that a large output of coins is possible, but rough handling is the price paid for speed. Electrically driven presses vomit forth coins at a tremendous rate and these fall into metal buckets where they jangle together and scratch each other. Thus it is no longer possible to speak of 'mint state' when referring to an uncirculated coin. There was quite an outcry in 1965, for

PLATE II

BRITISH COMMONWEALTH COINS

(1) Prince Edward Island 1c.; (2) Guernsey 12 doubles; (3) Ceylon ½c.; (4, 6) British Guiana; (5) Indian Empire; (7–8) Canada 1c., 5c.; (9) Malaya and British Borneo 10c.; (10, 12) Silver 1½d. coins used in Malta; (11) Half-farthing used in Ceylon; (13) Jersey 3d.; (14) Guernsey 10s.; (15) Guernsey 3d.

example, over the condition of the Churchill crowns which was generally poorer than one would normally expect of the Royal Mint. The extremely low relief of the reverse (portraying Churchill) seemed to lend itself more readily to damage during production. In a case such as this one would have no alternative but to accept a coin with *some* scratches on its surfaces—though as few as possible.

Before Boulton and Watt invented the steam-driven coin press in the 1790s coins were milled in a more leisurely fashion and usually retrieved from the press one by one by hand, so that a 'mint' coin would, indeed, be in that stage of perfection most desirable to a numismatist. Although with the passage of time this condition, known to collectors as *fleur de coin* (abbreviated to F.D.C.), is not common, it is by no means unheard of and there is nothing more calculated to warm the numismatic breast than the sight of a Greek tetradrachm or a Roman denarius in perfect, flawless condition, its surfaces mellowed with the patina of the centuries.

At this juncture, having mentioned patina, it might be advisable to say something about this feature of coins. Put at its crudest it might be termed as rust, but in the case of silver and copper coins this oxidation caused by exposure to the atmosphere or chemicals in the soil, is a protective coating which prevents further damage to the coin. Coins made of iron, zinc, lead and tin do not patinate gracefully, as has been noted earlier in this chapter. With copper, which often takes on a green, reddish-brown or even black patina, the appearance is usually enhanced. Silver darkens with age, while I have seen specimens which have acquired an attractive steel-blue tinge from chemicals in the dyes of velvet-lined presentation cases. Gold and platinum, which are virtually inert, do not patinate but have a lustre which withstands the passage of time.

On no account should the collector attempt to polish off the patina. Coins *can* be cleaned, using mild citric acid (lemon juice) for gold, or warm soapy water for silver, but if in doubt cleaning should not be attempted at all. Polishing coins to make them 'brighter' is vandalism of the worst order. Such well-meaning but thoroughly misplaced action automatically knocks 90% off the value of the coin. The same effect can be obtained by punching a hole in it—and no collector in his right mind would do that!

The only modern coins likely to turn up in true F.D.C. condition are proofs. These are specially minted coins, struck from special dies with a high finish, often of precious metal and on presses operating at a greatly reduced speed in order to keep accidental damage to the coins to an absolute minimum. Some modern gold proofs have their raised surfaces frosted in attractive contrast to their fields which have a mirror finish. Sometimes, where a coin is produced in cupro-nickel for normal circulation, proofs are struck in silver (e.g. the Bhutanese sertums of 1966). Invariably proofs are very much rarer than the normal issue, though occasionally certain coins only exist in proof form.

F.D.C. is synonymous with the American term Brilliant Uncirculated (often abbreviated to B.Unc. or B.U.) which is met with more frequently these days in dealers' lists and catalogues. Below this grade comes Uncirculated (Unc.) which indicates a coin in as perfect condition as is compatible with modern coining techniques. Extremely fine (E.F.) denotes a condition which is almost perfect, in a coin which has had a certain amount of handling but shows only minimal signs of wear on its highest surface. Very Fine (V.F.) is a term which, like coinage in general, has tended to become somewhat debased over the years. It is used to indicate a coin whose design, while still distinct, is showing definite signs of wear in its more prominent surfaces. On a penny, for example, the lines on the Union Jack would be clear, but not as sharp as possible, the folds in Britannia's dress and the waves of the sea would be rather faint, though the lettering, the date and the beading would be fairly sharp. Coins in V.F. condition are collectable if no better specimens are easily obtainable and there is sometimes a temptation to purchase coins in this grade in order to fill gaps. But it must be emphasised that, at present, money spent on modern coins in this condition is a false economy since they are not likely to appreciate in value at anything like the same rate that E.F. or Uncirculated specimens would—if, indeed, they did not actually lose money on re-sale.

Below this grade coins are not really worth considering unless they are rare in any case. Coins from the classical or medieval periods may be unobtainable in V.F.–Unc. condition, but modern coins must not be collected in lower grades. Dealers do not usually sell most modern items in the lower grades, but all too often one finds coins being offered in antique or junk shops in conditions which no self-respecting numismatist would pay for. I have seen badly worn coins, which catalogue at, say, £5 in E.F. condition, offered at £2 10s., when in fact 5s. expended on them would be a complete waste of money. When coins are scarce in any condition, however, the lower grades have to be taken into consideration.

Fine (F.) denotes a coin in worn condition, though the basic outline of the design may still be clear. On a penny, for example, the fine lines of the dress and the shield would be worn smooth and barely distinct while the lettering and figures would be coarsened though still legible.

Very Good (V.G.) is a euphemism which has become so debased as to mean the exact opposite! On a penny little would now be seen of the finer detail and the portions of the design in high relief, such as the lighthouse, ship and Britannia's helmet, would be flattened out. Finer details in the shield, robes and waves of the sea would have begun to disappear.

Good (G.) condition is, in fact, bad condition. A penny of this grade would be worn smooth all over; the outline of Britannia would be barely distinct while the finer details would have virtually vanished altogether. The date would just be readable and no more—and for this reason collectors will occasionally keep a coin in such bad condition when a particular year is uncommon.

From time to time publicity is given in the lay press to the rarity and value of pennies struck by Ralph Heaton of Birmingham and the King's Norton Mint who held contracts from the Royal Mint to do so at the end of the First World War. Pennies dated 1918 or 1919 with the tiny letters H or KN in the exergue, to the left of the date, are now worth from £20 to £60 in F.D.C. condition, but a dealer will sell specimens in V.G. condition for only a shilling or two.

Nevertheless it is astonishing the number of times that a non-collector, hearing of my interest in numismatics, will produce a well-worn penny with the coveted mint-marks barely discernible and state, with all the pride that ownership of a major rarity conveys, that the coin is worth a king's ransom. The pathetic belief in the value of H and KN pennies must be quite widespread, to the constant annoyance of the numismatic trade. At any rate there never seems to be a time, when I am visiting one or other of the shops in Great Portland Street, that some optimist does not wander in clutching his (or her) battered copper, with the reverence due to a Syracusan dekadrachm, and demand to know what the dealer will offer for it. Incidentally, the story of these coins' value tends to get somewhat garbled in the retelling and dealers are often plagued by the proud possessors of *any* 1918 or 1919 pennies though, without the sub-contractor's mint-marks, these are worth little more than their face value even in comparatively good condition.

Strange as it may seem, there are three grades of condition even lower than Good. These are, in descending order of desirability, Fair, Mediocre and Poor. Such terms have become so debased as to become virtually synonymous in practice, though Poor is a term which one would probably reserve for a coin which was not only scarcely identifiable but badly damaged—holed, chipped or scratched.

Inevitably, the grades listed above do not in themselves permit of the subtle, almost imperceptible shading from one into the other, so it is sometimes necessary to modify them. Thus between F.D.C. and E.F. one might find 'nearly F.D.C.' and 'Good E.F.', while the Americans use such expressions as 'About Uncirculated' (A.U.) and 'E.F. plus' to indicate these conditions respectively. Alternatively one may find two grades hyphenated (e.g. V.F.–E.F.) to indicate a condition better than Very Fine but not quite Extremely Fine.

Where only one grade is given for a coin it must be assumed that both obverse and reverse are of similar condition. Where, as sometimes happens, one side is in better condition than the other an oblique stroke between two grades (e.g. V.F./E.F.) indicates that the obverse is Very Fine while the reverse is Extra Fine. It is important not only to be able to understand precisely what is meant by these terms, when used in dealers' lists, auction lots and advertisements, but to assign a coin to its correct grading; otherwise a great deal of misunderstanding may arise or—what is much worse—you may end up by paying more for a coin than it is really worth.

It would not be out of place at this point to mention the scales of rarity used in describing coins. At one time the expressions 'rare', 'very rare', 'scarce' or 'common' were used indiscriminately in a vague, general manner to convey some idea of the relative scarcity of a coin but such a haphazard system was found to be far too imprecise for modern collecting. Credit must be given to B. A. Seaby Ltd. of London for evolving a table of comparative rarity which can be very exact:

R7 Unique or at most two examples known
R6 Three or four copies known
R5 Five to ten examples known
R4 Eleven to twenty examples known
R3 Extremely rare
R2 Very rare
R Rare
S Scarce
N Normal, neither scarce nor common
C Common
C2 Very common
C3 Extremely common

ERRORS AND VARIETIES

Philately, compared with numismatics, is a brash youngster and one of the facets of the former which appear somewhat infantile to the layman is the astonishing obsession for the imperfect. This pre-occupation is fortunately minimal so far as numismatics is concerned and, for the vast majority of serious collectors, an error in the production of a coin is of little importance unless it has some bearing on the production and eventual circulation of the coin. Thus mis-strikes which give a double or faulty impression on a coin are regarded as freaks possessing no more than curiosity value.

In the same category are brockages, caused by a coin adhering to the die during striking and thereby transferring its image to another blank which thus receives two impressions of the punch, one of which is normal (in relief) while the other is abnormal (incuse from the previous coin). In spite of the accuracy with which newly-minted coins are checked for defects, brockages and mis-strikes occasionally get into circulation. Other curiosities are split coins. These come about when a small air bubble, in the metal used for coining, is flattened out by the action of the rollers which produce the strips for punching out coin blanks. The air inside the disc causes it to split on impact with the punch and die of the press, though sometimes the split does not take place till the coin has got into circulation. Split coins of this sort likewise have little more than curiosity value.

The only errors in coining which can be regarded as valuable from a numismatic viewpoint are coins struck in the wrong metal, or coins struck from the correct punch and the wrong die (or *vice versa*). In modern issues, where coins are produced by the million, it is sometimes necessary to employ several dies and these may have some minute variations, insignificant to the officials of the mint and to the general public but of great importance to numismatists. A glance at C. W. Peck's magnificent *English Copper, Tin and Bronze Coins in the British Museum* reveals the scope there is in modern die variants. Normally one set of dies would be used for one coin throughout its minting, but occasionally the dies are transposed—one must suppose inadvertently—and the result is what numismatists term a 'mule'—a hybrid with the obverse die of one set and the reverse die of another. The converse situation may also arise and, consequently, where several sets of dies are used, the numbers of possible combinations of obverse and reverse is quite large. 'Mules' of this sort are of interest to the specialist collector and, unless they are as common as the normal variety, they usually command a considerable premium.

Coins struck in the wrong metals may be sub-divided into deliberate and accidental occurrences. In the first category come the experimental types produced by a mint when the introduction of a new metal or alloy is under consideration. The King's Norton mint in Birmingham, which was operated by Nobel Industries (a subsidiary of I.C.I.), conducted a number of experiments in the 1920s to investigate the practicability of using pure nickel and out of these experiments came the British shillings dated 1923 and 1924 struck in pure nickel instead of .500 silver. These experimental pieces are very scarce and fetch considerable sums when they turn up on the market. D. L. F. Sealy, discussing coin varieties of this type (*Coins and Medals*, February 1967), records a hitherto unknown cent of British East Africa, 1924 KN, struck in nickel (instead of bronze) and double the usual thickness. Other coins which are known to have been experimentally struck in metals other than the normal include a British farthing of Queen Anne (in lead instead of copper), the penny, halfpenny and farthing of 1868 (in cupro-nickel instead of bronze) and the penny and halfpenny of Jamaica released in the same year (in bronze instead of cupro-nickel). These mint trials are known to collectors as 'patterns', a term which is used to denote any coin of an experimental nature, including those whose designs or denominations were not subsequently adopted and put into circulation.

Mr. Sealy also records several instances of accidental usage of the wrong metal. This occurs where more than one type of coin is in production in a mint at the same time and the coin blanks intended for the one are inadvertently struck with the dies of another. Among recent errors of this sort have been recorded a British 6d. of 1966 in bronze (using the blank of a Dominican Republic centavo), a British threepence in cupro-nickel (Irish sixpence blank) and Nigerian shilling of 1961 in brass instead of cupro-nickel (Jamaican halfpenny blank).

A 10c. of British East Africa (1939 KN) which would normally be struck in bronze, was found in circulation, with its surfaces considerably worn so that traces of a white metal had begun to show through. On closer inspection it was discovered that the coin had in fact been minted in cupro-nickel (on the blank of a British West Africa penny). It would appear that the wrong blank had been included with a batch of bronze blanks at the blanching stage and, in being churned round with them in an acid solution, became plated with copper. This would have disguised it effectively so that it was struck and put into circulation in the normal way, without being detected for many years till wear revealed its true composition.

One of the most curious 'mules' of recent times got into circulation in 1967 when the New Zealand decimal coins were introduced. A quantity of the 2c. denomination was struck at the Royal Mint with the correct reverse used but, by accident, the obverse die for the Bahamas 5c. was used instead. This bears a profile of the Queen and the inscription ELIZABETH II BAHAMA ISLANDS. Some 100,000 of these curiosities actually reached New Zealand and approximately 2,000 vanished into circulation before the authorities noticed the error and suppressed the issue. Those that were not rounded up were changing hands within two days of their release for anything up to $50 (£20) and since then the market value of the New Zealand mule has risen considerably.

Apart from brockages, mis-strikes and mules, a relatively common type of error consists of mis-spelling in the inscriptions —particularly in the hammered coinage of medieval times. This sort of mistake has been recorded on quite modern pieces, however, and is brought about by the separate entry of letters or figures (particularly the latter, in dates) on the die. Figures may be found irregularly spaced or struck twice or one figure struck on top of another to correct an error in the date. Such errors are of definite numismatic interest, so it pays the student to be ever-vigilant.

CHAPTER III

GOLD

GOLD has always had a special place in the estimation of mankind. Its virtual incorruptibility and eternal lustre have combined to make it the most highly and universally regarded of the precious metals. Jewellery fashioned of gold before the dawn of history has been excavated from the soil, gleaming as brightly as when it did countless thousands of years ago.

Until fairly recent times most countries had a gold standard coinage and, although Britain had to abandon its gold standard in 1931 when the pound sterling suffered the first of its modern devaluations, sovereigns and half sovereigns are still legal tender. A country's economic strength is measured in terms of its gold reserves and, in post-war Britain at least, it was found to be necessary to place some restriction on the movement of gold, in order to prevent hoarding by private individuals or a drain abroad of the country's gold. The gold sovereign, nominally worth 20s., now has an intrinsic value at least four times that amount. In 1947, however, the value of a sovereign in the French black market was more than 100s. and the following year it actually rose as high as 128s.

Obviously it would therefore have been an extremely lucrative proposition for speculators in Britain to export sovereigns to France and profit by the high prices obtained there. The British government, however, made such a proposition illegal by introducing the Exchange Control Act in 1947 which laid down that 'no person other than an authorised dealer should buy, borrow, lend or sell any gold or foreign currency.' Moreover it was stipulated that 'any person possessing gold should offer it for sale to an authorised dealer at a price not exceeding the authorised price, unless the Treasury consented to his retention of the gold.' This Act would have posed serious problems for the numismatist, had not the Exchange Control (Collectors' Pieces Exemption) Order 1947 been brought into force simultaneously. This allowed collectors to hold on to 'any gold coin which was minted in 1816 or earlier, and any gold coin which was minted after 1816 and which has a numismatic value greater than the value of the gold content which would have been received if the coin had been sold to an authorised (bullion) dealer.' In effect this meant that numismatists and coin dealers were not hindered from buying and selling gold coins as long as the coins were in collectable condition and possessed numismatic interest.

No check was made on numismatists to see that they kept to the regulations, however, and it has to be conceded that a great amount of trading was engaged in in recent years in sovereigns *per se* and not as collectors' pieces. By the mid-1960s interest in gold as a hedge against inflation had risen to unprecedented heights and advertisements appeared quite openly (in the Personal columns of the 'quality' Sunday newspapers, for example) offering sovereigns for £3 10s. each or as little as £320 for a hundred.

This blatant disregard of the terms of the 1947 Act and its attendant Exemption Order coincided with a remarkable phenomenon which can only be described as the 'gold medal craze'. Some experts aver that the craze began in 1964 with the Shakespeare quatercentenary medals struck in gold which were heavily over subscribed and rose in value at a meteoric rate. My own feeling, however, is that the boom in these expensive gold commemorative pieces was touched off a year earlier, when the Polynesian kingdom of Tonga released a set of three gold coins—the first indigenous gold coinage from the Pacific islands.

On 22nd April, 1963, the coins, in denominations of one, half and quarter koulas (*koula* being the Tongan word for gold), went into circulation. Great stress was laid, at the time, on the fact that these were the first gold coins placed into circulation at their face value as part of a nation's currency since the

world-wide abandonment of the gold standard more than thirty
years previously. The koula (with a face value of £16 sterling,
£20 in Australian funds) was naively described as the highest
denomination of any gold coin placed in actual circulation for
almost two centuries, but when it is realised that £16 represented slightly more than the average annual income in Tonga
it will be seen that very few of these large and handsome pieces
could ever have passed from hand to hand in the course of
normal business transactions in Polynesia!

The quantities minted were very small (1,500 koula, 3,000
half koula and 6,300 quarter koula, together with a minute
quantity of proofs). Originally sets could be obtained from
the Crown Agents in London at £28 10s. the additional 10s.
covering the cost of an attractive velvet-lined leather case) but
the orders received by the Crown Agents far exceeded the
supply, so that sets had to be balloted for. The publicity given
to this issue was naturally great and the Tongan gold coins
were enormously popular from the outset, with the result that
the price rose rapidly to £150.

This was some indication of the thirst for modern gold pieces
which was to spread the following year when the 400th anniversary of the birth of William Shakespeare was marked by a
medal struck by the Italian medallists, Aurea Numismatica.

The fashion for commemorative medals in gold spread
rapidly from the Continent where a rash of these pieces appeared about this time. Among the earliest pieces were medals
depicting famous composers (Mozart, Schubert and Johann
Strauss), those with a religious flavour (Popes Paul VI and
John XXIII in commemoration of the Ecumenical Council)
and one acknowledging the arrival of the Space Age (with
portraits of scientists, Copernicus, Keppler, Newton and
Einstein on the obverse and the cosmonauts, Glenn, Cooper,
Schirra and Carpenter on the reverse). M. & F. Feuchtwanger,
the merchant bankers, who were sole distributors in the United
Kingdom, advertised these items in the numismatic press
in September 1964 under the slogan 'Invest in 18 carat Gold
Hallmarked Medallions' and it has to be conceded that any-
body who purchased them at the time of the offer and sold

them a year later made a handsome profit on the venture, although, as a long-term investment, such medals have not turned out quite so well.

In 1965 came a spate of medals in memory of Sir Winston Churchill who died in January of that year. They were preceded slightly by a set of three gold medals struck by the Swiss Credit Bank, from designs by Professor R. Schmidt of Vienna, in honour of Churchill's 90th birthday the previous November. The Schmidt medals were minted in a limited edition and soon were changing hands for sums in excess of £100—well above the intrinsic value of the gold itself. B. A. Seaby Ltd. of London re-issued the Lowenthal medal (struck originally in bronze in 1946) in gold as a memorial to Churchill. Not to be out-done, Spink's of London also produced a Churchill medal in two sizes, the larger retailing at £100 and the smaller at £35. Other Churchill medals (with their prices in parentheses) were produced by Ironside (£170), L. A. Kaitcer (£155), Gregory (£110) and Pinches (£96). Other medals followed thick and fast—commemorating President Kennedy, the anniversary of El Alamein (with portraits of Rommel and Montgomery), the Sark Royal Charter and Albert Schweitzer, not to mention the prolific coin-medals of Israel and a lengthy series of gold reproductions of classic postage stamps, manufactured by Numismatica Italiana in an attempt to convert stamp-collectors to numismatics! Even the Isle of Man government jumped on the band-wagon by issuing gold £5 pieces, sovereigns and half-sovereigns which found a ready sale at £100 a set. Several firms sprang up rapidly and during 1965 and early 1966 business boomed as the gold medals proliferated.

The ultimate seemed to have arrived, with an ambitious series of gold medals planned in 1966 to portray the Prime Ministers of Britain since Walpole, when suddenly the Government pricked the gold bubble by introducing the Exchange Control (Gold Coins Exemption) Order 1966. The object of the order, which came into effect on 27th April, 1966, was to prevent the loss of currency reserves caused by the import of gold coins and medals from abroad and to eliminate the hoarding of gold by speculators as opposed to genuine coin collectors, who nevertheless were now to be subject to strict control.

By the terms of this Order no-one was permitted to hold more than four gold coins minted after 1837 unless they had received express permission from the Treasury. The maximum was set at four coins so that people who had one or two sovereigns as mementoes of palmier days could keep them without breaking the law. The date 1837 is a curious one, chosen no doubt since it coincides with the accession of Queen Victoria, but this in itself seems insufficient reason, since *foreign* gold coins after this date come under the interdict and, in this context, the year 1837 is meaningless. The order has given rise to a nonsensical situation; the Treasury maintain on the one hand that sovereigns and half-sovereigns are still legal tender but, on the other hand, now make it illegal for the average British citizen to possess them.

Numismatists who possessed more than four post-1837 gold coins on 27th April, 1966, had to apply to the Treasury for permission to retain them. To do so they had to prove that they were *bona fide* collectors by completing form G.C.1 which is in itself an interesting document. Just as 'instant legislation' had now made any normally law-abiding citizen a criminal if he possessed more than the statutory four coins, so also the form required from the numismatist fairly precise details of his collection. Each post-1837 gold coin held at present has to be listed with a detailed description. The purpose of this inquisition is obvious, but the form then goes on to demand the number and approximate value of the pre-1838 gold coins in the collection. Moreover, holdings of silver coins minted after 1919, between 1816 and 1919, and before 1816, as well as base metal coins before and after 1860, have to be disclosed, the object of this apparently being to prove to the satisfaction of the Treasury the genuineness of one's numismatic interests, although one may see in this prying something more ominous.

Nothing could be more calculated to destroy one's pleasure in a hobby than all this form-filling and bureaucratic interference. B.A. Seaby Ltd. quote one of their lady customers as writing about it as 'an obscene indignity' and most other collectors have expressed their feelings on these lines, if not quite so strongly. It is a matter for some conjecture just how many numismatists have ceased to collect gold coins rather than make a declaration which is against their principles. By the mere stroke of the legislator's pen many decent, law-abiding citizens have run the risk of becoming law-breakers.

The mere application on form G.C.1 does not, however, confer an automatic right to authorisation from the Bank of England to keep or collect gold coins. The ways of the Bank are like the peace of God, they pass all understanding, and there is no telling what are the criteria which its officials in their infinite wisdom apply to those seeking authorisation. Nowhere are the rules for qualification set out and it appears that, in spite of the Bank's assurances to the contrary, some *bona fide* collectors have had their applications turned down. Moreover the division of the 'haves' from the 'have-nots' is distressingly apparent; collectors who have hitherto confined their activities to silver and base-metal coins but who now wish to collect post-1837 gold have, in many cases, been turned down. Some curiously naive advice has been given to them; it has been suggested that they make a start by acquiring some pre-1837 gold coins and then apply again at a later date to take up post-1837 pieces. The worst aspect of all this, however, is that the numismatist whose application has been turned down has no right of appeal to a higher authority.

Those who do secure the Bank's permission to collect post-1837 gold do so only on the condition that they may not keep more than two examples of any given coin (different dates, mint marks and die variations being regarded as distinct types). Any duplicates above that number have to be sold to an author-ised dealer. It cannot be denied that the effect of such forced sales has gravely affected the market.

In the rigorous attempt to control gold collecting the Treasury has made no distinction between ordinary specie used as a medium of exchange on the international market and items of pure numismatic interest, such as proofs and patterns, which cannot be regarded as part of the nation's gold reserves. Yet post-1837 coins which have been mounted for use as cuff-links, brooches or bracelets are deemed to be jewellery and, as such, are exempt from the 1966 Order. It is difficult to understand why rare coins should be treated so differently.

Authorisation to collect post-1837 gold coins takes the form of a letter from the Bank of England confirming that permission has been given. Collectors can exchange or buy coins from other collectors provided both parties concerned have a licence, but to buy or sell privately they have to apply to the Bank for permission. When purchasing coins from a dealer the letter of authorisation has to be produced in the first instance.

The possession of gold medals is not apparently affected, but the purchase of such items is now forbidden and the manufacture of them has virtually come to a stand-still.

What are the effects of this drastic move on the part of the Treasury? The first and most immediate has been to undermine the position of London as the centre of the world coin market. This enviable position, built up by collectors of taste and discrimination on the one hand, and honest and experienced dealers and auctioneers on the other, is in serious danger of being destroyed. Hitherto London was favoured for the sale of internationally famous collections because of the comparative lack of restriction on the entry and exit of gold coins, but now the present regulations are bound to have an adverse effect. The annual turnover in the London coin market runs to several millions, a good proportion of which contributed to the international balance of payments. It is a sad commentary on the uneasy economic situation of the United Kingdom that, at a time when other countries are strengthening their economic position and confidence in non-gold currencies—producing a powerful disincentive to gold hoarding—the British Treasury apparently finds it necessary to take such desperate action to prop up a shaky economy.

The Opposition were not long in tabling a prayer to annul the Order but this was defeated in the House of Commons on 13th July, 1966, by 169 votes to 94. Stringent penalties, including fines, imprisonment and the confiscation of the collection could be invoked for offences against the Order, but as is not uncommon in the administration of the law in this country, the treatment of offenders has not been consistent.

The first prosecution brought under the 1966 Order occurred on 18th January, 1967, when a garage owner, Mr. Frederick Knight, of Mevagissey, Cornwall, was charged with failing to disclose his collection of 703 gold coins and, while not being an authorised dealer, he failed to offer them for sale to an authorised dealer. Mr. Knight, who pleaded guilty, was fined £50 and an order for the disposal of the collection at the behest of the Treasury was made. In addition he was fined £5 for failing to offer 54 United States dollars for sale to an authorised dealer. His defending counsel said that this was not a question of hoarding, adding, 'His father and grandfather, and a person to whom he was kind, left him their collections. It is hard to imagine a more genuine collection of coins ranging from Elizabethan times to the present. This legislation has all the aspects of retrospective legislation. Mr. Knight did what was perfectly legal for 40 years and then, by the stroke of a pen in April, 1966, it became illegal to have what he had collected. I ask you to say that this was as far from hoarding gold as Mr. Knight is from being King Midas.'

The prosecution accepted that this was a genuine collection. Presumably the fact that Mr. Knight had this collection was not exactly a secret, for the local police got to hear of it and, obtaining a search warrant, took possession of 714 gold coins—eleven of which were found to be counterfeit and therefore not covered by the Order. The Treasury were lenient in that a forfeiture order was not pressed and they were content merely to insist that the collection, a life-time's accumulation, be disposed of to an authorised dealer. Mr. Knight's counsel commented that to apply the penalties designed to prevent gold hoarding was a classic example of taking a sledge hammer to crack a walnut. He added that the Treasury had selected the hapless Mr. Knight as a guinea pig, 'so that people will know they can be prosecuted for this'.

A second prosecution followed ten days later when Mr. Fortunato Fenech of Hackney, London, pleaded guilty to possessing 738 gold sovereigns without being an authorised

PLATE III

British Commonwealth Coins

(1) Rhodesia 2s./20c.; (2) Malawi florin; (3) India 'Nehru' rupee; (4) Zambia 2s.;
(5) Australia florin; (6) Australia 20c.; (7) New Zealand florin; (8) Southern
Rhodesia halfcrown; (9) East Africa shilling; (10) Nigeria shilling; (11) Cyprus
100m.; (12) Australian shilling.

dealer and without offering them for sale to a dealer. The defendant admitted quite frankly that he had hoarded the sovereigns as a form of savings, but that he was quite unaware of the 1966 Order making such a practice illegal. The magistrate, Mr. Frank Milton, told Fenech, 'I accept that you didn't know a new law was made. That being so I am not going to punish you.' He was given a year's conditional discharge and no order was made regarding the disposal of the coins.

Ignorance of the law is not usually argued as a defence and a comparison of the punishment meted out to a genuine collector on the one hand and a professed hoarder on the other could afford interesting discussion on the inconsistency of justice done in British magistrates' courts, but this would be quite futile here.

Another repercussion of the gold restriction has been an increase in the use of the platinum group of metals which, from the point of view of intrinsic value, are more precious than gold and do not suffer the disadvantages to which gold is subject at present. Although platinum has been used in the production of coins for at least two centuries it has never been popular, except with counterfeiters. Platinum did not begin to rise to its present relative value till industrial and scientific applications in the late nineteenth century created an enormous demand for it. Before that time it was comparatively cheap and because its specific gravity was akin to gold it encouraged forgers to imitate gold coins.

One of the very few collectors of platinum pieces, Nick Parker, had an unusual experience which illustrates very well the problem of counterfeits facing the numismatist. A fellow-collector once purchased a 2 peso gold coin of the Philippines, 1864, which, although in fine condition, appeared to be rather dirty. He attempted to clean it with aqua regia acid in the approved manner, but was appalled to find the gold colouring dissolving, thus revealing the piece as a counterfeit. Justifiably he returned it to the dealer from whom it had been purchased and he in turn passed it over to Mr. Parker as a platinum counterfeit. As traces of the gilding still adhered to it, he decided to remove them thoroughly in aqua regia. This not only took off the gilding but also removed the silver colouring—

to reveal an apparently genuine gold coin. It would seem that a previous owner had silver-plated the gold coin for use on jewellery. This might have been the end of the story if Nick Parker had not given the coin yet another application of the acid. The gold colouring again dissolved and there, at last, was a platinum counterfeit!

Apart from forgery, platinum was used in the production of proofs and patterns, the earliest being struck by the Colombian Mint as long ago as 1763. The Spanish mints in South America, where platinum was mined, conducted a number of experiments and the mother country herself produced several attractive patterns down till the early years of this century. The United States, France and Germany have also produced platinum proofs or patterns at one time or another but, until recently, the only country to mint coins for general circulation was Russia where the metal was discovered (in the Ural Mountains) in 1824. Two years later a pattern half rouble was struck in platinum and between 1828 and 1830 coins in denominations of 3, 6 and 12 roubles were minted in this metal. The increased output of the Siberian mines, however, led to the inevitable slump in the market and platinum, which had enjoyed a brief popularity as an alternative to gold, suffered disastrously and public antipathy to the platinum coins forced their withdrawal from circulation by 1845. It has been estimated that altogether about 1,500,000 platinum pieces got into circulation; of these few remain in the hands of collectors and are consequently highly prized today.

Then in July 1967 Tonga, which had done so much to precipitate the ephemeral craze for gold, came up with a new plan aimed at beating the British gold restrictions. The Coronation of His Majesty, King Taufa' Ahau Tupou IV was marked by the release of a set of seven coins ranging in denomination from 20 seniti (cents) to 1 hau (the Tongan equivalent of 'sovereign'). The four lowest denominations were struck in cupro-nickel, while the $\frac{1}{4}$, $\frac{1}{2}$ and 1 hau pieces were minted in palladium, one of the six 'platinum metals'. The largest of these coins was equal to £40 sterling, was $1\frac{3}{4}''$ in diameter and weighed 1,000 Imperial grains, thus making it the largest, heaviest and most valuable coin produced since the end of the eighteenth century. No more than 1,500 of the 1 hau were minted, so that the number of complete sets was restricted to that figure and, like the humbler koula, it obviously never circulated in the Pacific Island kingdom—if at all.

Already several commemorative medals have been released in platinum, at exorbitant prices, and have begun to attract the attention of the hoarder rather than the serious collector. Could history repeat itself and are we heading for similar Government restrictions regarding this once unpopular metal?

CHAPTER IV

COLLECTING COINS

APART from acquisition by gift, the main methods of obtaining coins are in change, by exchange and by purchase, either from another collector or, more usually, through a dealer or auctioneer. The first of these methods has come to the fore in recent years with the spread from America of the practice of collecting modern coins and attempting to build up complete sets according to date and mint marks. This practice is rapidly transforming us into a nation of 'change-checkers'; people pause now, when tendering their fare on a bus or paying for groceries, to make sure that no rare dates—no 1952 sixpence or 1918 KN penny—escapes into the conductor's wallet or the shopkeeper's till.

To ease the task of remembering which are the scarce items not to let by, Rotographic Ltd. have produced a tiny pamphlet of 32 pages (five inches by three) which fits easily into the handbag or wallet. Entitled *Check Your Change*, it gives the bare essentials—numbers minted and 1967 market valuation—for all British coins since 1902 in circulation. Coins prior to that date, but which are still likely to be met with in business or shopping, are covered by a second booklet, *Check Your Victorian Change*, while a third volume deals with coins not in circulation—sovereigns, half sovereigns, Maundy money and farthings.

Another handy *aide memoire* is *Pocket Money*, recently published by *Coins, Medals and Currency*, the weekly numismatic newspaper.

It would be impossible to remember *all* the scarce dates, mint-marks and dies of modern British coins but the following list includes the more elusive items which are worth laying aside, provided that they are in Very Good condition at least.

Halfpennies:	1902 low tide, 1946, 1953.
Pennies:	1902 low tide, 1912 H, 1918 H/KN, 1919 H/KN, 1926 (modified head), 1950, 1951, 1953.
Silver Threepences:	1942, 1943, 1944.
Brass Threepences:	1936 (King Edward VIII), 1946, 1949.
Sixpences:	1902–10, 1923, 1952.
Shillings:	1902–10, 1930, 1938 (E,S), 1939 (E,S), 1959 (S), 1961 (S).
Florins:	1902–10, 1932.
Halfcrowns:	1902–10, 1930.

The significance of the H and KN mint has already been explained in Chapter II. The so-called 'Low Tide' and 'Modified Head' coins exhibit die variations which are comparatively scarce, but a little practice may be required in order to distinguish them from the commoner types of the same date. As a compliment to Queen Elizabeth (now the Queen Mother) and as a tribute to her Scottish origins, distinctive Scottish shillings were minted from 1937 onwards. This practice has been continued up to the present time. In the Georgian series the lion sits on the crown, flanked by saltire cross and thistle (Scottish) or stands astride the crown (English), while in the Elizabethan series (1953 to date) the difference lies in the coats of arms on the reverse—three leopards (English) and lion rampant (Scottish).

Generally speaking, the Scottish shillings of the Georgian series are comparable in number to the English variety (indeed, in some years—1949 and 1951—they were more numerous). In the Elizabethan series, however, with the exception of 1958 (when 40 million Scottish shillings and only 14 million English shillings were minted) and 1966 (when approximately equal numbers were issued) the English variety are very much more common than the Scottish, though both are usually too plentiful

to make the disparity in numbers affect their numismatic value
to any appreciable degree.

The coins listed above are desirable in any condition from
Very Good upwards, but in the higher categories other coins
can be added to the list, including quite recent issues. At the
time of writing this book there is something of a boom in
halfcrowns, particularly those minted between 1954 and 1960
in EF or Uncirculated condition. According to a market survey
conducted by *Coins, Medals and Currency* (20th January, 1968)
the prices for certain dates doubled in two months, that is to
say, between the time immediately after the devaluation of
sterling and mid-January 1968. Prices of EF halfcrowns
remained static, but Uncirculated specimens increased dramatically in some cases. For example, 1954 coins doubled, from
£3 10s. to £7, while 1958 or 1959 halfcrowns went up from
25s. to £5—a 400% increase in eight weeks! That this market is
basically unstable, however, is indicated by the fact that, over
the same period, the price of Uncirculated 1955 halfcrowns *fell*
from £2 to 25s., and 1957 pieces dropped from 25s. to 17s.

Mention of halfcrowns brings me to a tale with a moral—it
always pays to check your change. It was as a result of this
habit that Mr. Horace Burrows of Chelmsford, Essex, discovered a halfcrown dated 1952, a date hitherto unrecorded. The
fact that the coin is only in Very Good condition indicates that
it must have seen a considerable amount of circulation in the
fifteen years before its discovery. Officially no halfcrowns were
held to exist with this date. On account of the death of King
George VI in February 1952, no halfcrowns bearing his effigy
were put into circulation that year. It appears, however, that
dies had been prepared and a few halfcrowns were struck from
them and must have subsequently, though inexplicably, got
into circulation. There is always a possibility, therefore, that
other examples of this coin may turn up.

This possibility may account for the element of anti-climax
in the subsequent history of this halfcrown. Its discovery was
widely publicised in the national press and figures up to £10,000
were set on it (this being the price allegedly paid for the only
other modern British coin thought to be unique—the 1954

penny formerly in the Peck Collection). The 1952 halfcrown was to be the highlight of an auction conducted by Mr. C. N. Richardson of the London Stamp Exchange, at the National Coin Exhibition staged in the Chenil Galleries, Chelsea on 7th September, 1967. In the event, however, it was knocked down at £1,600 and this disappointment was regarded at the time as a result of mismanagement of the auction which, for some unaccountable reason, began half an hour early, before the big dealers and wealthier collectors had had an opportunity to assemble. It subsequently transpired that the coin had *not* been sold, but had, in fact, been 'bought in' by the auctioneer on Mr. Burrows' behalf, when it failed to reach the reserve price of £2,000 set on it.

Mr. Burrows later advertised it for sale, through the Coin Tray column in *Coins, Medals and Currency*, for £2,000. This failed to elicit a buyer, but came to the attention of Dunns, the coin dealers of Norfolk, Virginia, who offered to list the coin in their next postal auction which took place on 21st February, 1968. The coin was entered with a reserve of $5,280 (£2,200) and has now apparently found a bidder at this price.

* * * * *

As one assembles a collection of modern coins from one's change certain patterns begin to emerge. Apart from the incidence or comparative rarity of certain dates one begins to note that certain denominations are less common than others. Halfpennies and shillings fall into this category. The halfpenny, which, since the farthing was demonetised in 1956, is now the smallest British coin in circulation, has now shrunk in value almost to the point of worthlessness so far as purchasing power is concerned. I doubt whether there is anything which one can purchase for a halfpenny these days, except a postage stamp which in itself serves no individual purpose. Consequently this coin is virtually restricted to change for odd amounts in payment of groceries and petrol. With its demonetisation in August 1969 it will vanish from the commercial scene entirely. The shilling, on the other hand, is a coin which performs a useful function and no doubt will continue to do so, for a few years at least. But though countless numbers have been minted in recent years (almost 700 millions since 1953 alone) comparatively few seem to be in circulation at any time, since most of them are rapidly swallowed up by slot machines, fuel meters and telephone boxes. Another reason which has been advanced to explain the unpopularity of this coin is the fact that, at most, only one would occur in a wage packet at any time (whereas three halfcrowns or four florins would be possible).

For the same reason the brass threepence is not as common as it used to be, while its use in slot-machines has been drastically reduced now that the minimum rate in coin-operated public telephones has been increased to 6d. Admittedly over 50 million 3d. coins were minted in 1966, but this figure was well up on editions for some years past, yet, at the same time, was less than half that of the peak years during the Second World War. Incidentally, roughly half a million threepenny pieces were minted in 1946 and 1949, thus making these items two of the rarest of the regularly issued British coins in recent years.

It may seem strange, but there is an apparent divergence in the regional distribution of coins throughout the country. In large cities, such as London, Birmingham and Glasgow, where coinage has a high rate of turnover, the majority of coins now in circulation bear the effigy of Queen Elizabeth. At the other extreme, while living in the Outer Hebrides for three years, I was often struck by the high incidence of pre-war coins in VF–EF condition while Victorian and Edwardian silver was by no means uncommon. This phenomenon can be accounted for by the traditional distrust of the crofter in banks and a conservative reliance on a 'sockful of siller' under the floor instead of a savings account. Digressing for a moment, I recall the bank manager, on the island where I was living, telling me of an old lady who responded to a Spitfire Fund appeal during the war by producing a hundred notes of the City of Glasgow Bank. Her family had hoarded them for many years, apparently unaware that this bank had crashed in the latter years of the nineteenth century!

Even nearer to 'civilisation', a friend of mine, who is employed as a rent collector for a rural district council in Shropshire, took up numismatics as a result of handling old coins in the course of his work and in less than six months had put together an astonishing collection of pre-1920 silver coins in remarkably fine condition. A great many minor hoards of treasure trove may have been nothing more than the life savings of long-vanished generations, from an age when banks were few and far between, and when business was by barter and specie was not handled so frequently.

NUMISMATIC SOCIETIES

If one relied entirely on coins acquired in change, one's collection would never progress beyond the superficial, sketchy stage and an embryonic interest in numismatics would inevitably die unless nurtured and stimulated further by contact with other collectors. For this reason it is essential for the budding numismatist to join a society or club and, with more than sixty of them in Britain now, there is bound to be one within reasonable distance. By coming in contact with other, more experienced numismatists the novice's interests are developed and his standards of observation and critical study are raised.

Most societies meet once a month and their annual programmes consist partly of lectures and displays by visiting speakers of note in the numismatic world—leading members of the trade and curators of museum collections as well as private collectors—and partly in discussions by the members themselves. Displays of actual coins and medals are often accompanied by film-strips or slides and, for the most part, these lectures are very entertaining as well as edifying. A portion of the evening, however, is usually given up to informal chat among the members and this is the time when private buying, selling and exchanging takes place. Undoubtedly the most economic way of collecting coins is by dealing direct with a fellow-enthusiast but obviously this method, though mutually advantageous, has its limitations.

Likewise society auctions, usually held once a year, offer a useful medium for the disposal of one's duplicates at a fair price and the purchase of items for less than one might have to pay a dealer. Sooner or later, however, one has to consult a dealer or study catalogues of forthcoming auctions in order to fill those difficult gaps whose presence in the collection detracts from its value as a complete entity.

Dealers and auctioneers are considered in greater detail later on.

An enquiry at your local public library will determine whether there is a numismatic society in your district; if there is, the librarian will be able to furnish details of the meeting place, the programme of events and the address of the secretary. A list of those clubs which are affiliated to the British Association of Numismatic Societies is published in *Cunobelin*, the year book of the Association. This list is reproduced in Howard Linecar's recent *Beginner's Guide to Coin Collecting*, while a more comprehensive list appears as an appendix to *The Coin Collector's Encyclopaedia* compiled by Colin Narbeth. New societies are being formed so rapidly, however, that it pays to study the numismatic periodicals for details of the latest foundations. The most complete and up-to-date lists of numismatic societies in the United Kingdom appear in *Coins and Medals Annual* and *'Coin Monthly' Yearbook* published by the two leading commercial monthly magazines.

With the exception of the two senior national societies, the Royal and the British Numismatic Societies (both of which have an entrance fee of a guinea and an annual subscription of £4 4s. od.), the subscriptions to the majority of the coin clubs are well below £1. This modest outlay is amply repaid by the valuable experience gained from contact with other numismatists, to say nothing of the enrichment of one's enjoyment of the hobby.

DEALERS

Although the oldest-established coin dealer in Britain can claim to have been in business for more than three centuries this is a form of trading which has only begun to develop in a big way since the Second World War. Spink and Son of St. James's, London, were founded in 1666 and have built up an international reputation as fine art dealers, with a strong bias towards coins, medals and decorations. Apart from their preeminence in these fields Spink's often act as agents on behalf of the British government and overseas administrations in handling the numismatic sales of coins, invariably in 'cased sets' or as proofs. Spink's are also medallists in their own right (holding warrants from the Queen and the Duke of Edinburgh) and have been responsible for many fine examples of medallic art.

The only other firm of numismatic dealers established in this country more than fifty years ago is Baldwin's of the Adelphi, London, who cover all fields from classical Greek and Roman to modern British, Commonwealth and foreign coins. Next in chronological order comes B. A. Seaby Ltd. founded in 1926. The founder of this business, H. A. ('Bert') Seaby, began as a professional with Spink's shortly after the First World War and launched forth on his own at the time of the General Strike. In spite of this unpropitious beginning Seaby's rank undubitably in the Big Three and have, consciously or unconsciously, drawn many of the newer firms into their orbit so that Great Portland Street, where Bert Seaby set up shop many years ago, is now a mecca for coin collectors and is to the numismatic world what Savile Row is to the sartorially conscious.

Although the Big Three hold prodigious stocks of coins covering the globe from earliest times to the present day, the tendency with many of the newer firms has been to specialise in certain fields or periods. Thus the aptly named Maundy Allen of Great Portland Street specialises in Maundy money and Farthing Specialists of Bury, Lancs., are concerned exclusively with this humble coin from its inception in 1613 to its demise in 1956.

For crowns one would probably go to Carla Coins of Regent Street, E. H. R. Gilbert of Thundersley, Essex, or Southern Numismatists of Sittingbourne, Kent. Connoisseurs of fine coins in general would do well to approach Nick Parker of Knightsbridge or L. H. Gance of Hatton Garden while Stewart Ward of Great Portland Street concentrates on English hammered coinage. For 'moderns' two lady dealers carry extensive stocks —Joan Allen of Biggin Hill and Eva Hardy of The Coin Cabinet, Trafalgar Square. Space alone prevents me from mentioning other dealers in London and the Home Counties. Farther afield mention must be made of Corbitt and Hunter of Newcastle-upon-Tyne and the Leeds Coin Centre in the north-east, and J. A. Duggan of Blackburn in the north-west. Scotland's leading dealer is Michael Ferris of Glasgow, while L. A. Kaitcer of Belfast serves the numismatic needs of Ireland.

With the phenomental development of coin collecting in Britain, numismatic dealers have sprung up all over the country with astonishing rapidity. The great majority of them, fortunately, have entered the trade with a substantial experience of numismatics gained as amateur collectors and then as part-time traders, or, like D. J. Crowther of New Bond Street and Bert Seaby before him, have gained an invaluable training with one of the old-established firms and then set up in business on their own account. These dealers are honest and industrious, with reputations to protect and their customers' goodwill to foster, so that collectors can usually be assured of a fair deal from them. Like apples, however, one wrong 'un can taint the rest in the eyes of the lay public, so the trade has formed two organisations to regulate coin dealing and prevent dishonesty or malpractice.

The International Association of Professional Numismatists has the declared aim of 'bringing together expert numismatists of the entire world with the object of co-ordinating the work of the development and propagation of Numismatics.' The I.A.P.N. has set up a Service of Experts at the disposal of collectors, as well as an Information and Inquiries Service dealing with forgeries. All members of this Association are bound to guarantee the authenticity of coins sold by them. Dealers who infringe its code of ethics can be expelled, or barried from admission; conversely, the I.A.P.N. maintains a black-list of fraudulent collectors or bad debtors which is circulated to members for their protection. The headquarters of the I.A.P.N. are located at 7, Rue Drouot, Paris, from which a general list of members, published annually, may be obtainable.

The growth of the numismatic industry in Britain itself led to the formation in 1967 of the Professional Numismatists Association which regulates the conduct of the profession at the national level. The Secretary of the P.N.A. is Nick Parker, from whom details of member-dealers may be obtained.

Despite the efforts of these Associations there is still a rather shady fringe, mainly of part-time traders or 'antique-dealers' who charge excessive prices for mediocre specimens and pay a fraction of their true worth for desirable items. There is unfortunately little which can be done collectively to stamp out such malpractices. Greater dissemination of information alone can succeed in putting collectors or vendors on their guard and, to their credit, the general numismatic periodicals, especially *Coins, Medals and Currency*, have fearlessly exposed malpractices brought to their notice. More is said on this topic in Chapter XI.

Coins have never been retailed so universally as stamps, for example, which are sold in department stores and newsagents' shops as well as by specialised philatelic dealers. The sale of coins in large stores is an establi hed feature in the United States, however, and it has recentl; been introduced in Britain. In January of this year Harrods of Knightsbridge inaugurated a Coin Section, specialising in British copper and silver coins from the seventeenth century to the present, but carrying a good general stock including proof and specimen sets as well as numismatic accessories.

AUCTIONS

The most important source of material these days is the numismatic auction. Occasional sales of coins and medals are conducted in Britain by most of the provincial auctioneers and though these are seldom exclusively numismatic, being part of general sales including books, prints, furniture, *objets d'art* and antiques as a rule, it is surprising how often interesting items turn up at reasonable prices.

The collector who has taken the trouble to seek out the sale of the contents of a country house, perhaps, and has discovered one or two lots of numismatic interest, is often well rewarded for his efforts, and usually does not have any competition from professional numismatists; it being seldom worth their while to follow up a sale of this sort, often in out of the way districts, for the sake of the odd item of value.

There are barely a score of auction houses in the United Kingdom who handle coins and medals on a more regular basis and, although they sometimes have quite important items for disposal, attracting the close attention of serious numismatists as well as coin dealers, auctions consisting entirely of coins and medals are in the main confined to a handful of firms alone. Foremost in this field are Glendining & Co. Ltd. of Blenheim Street, London W.1, who hold sales regularly during the season. In recent years Christie's, the fine art auctioneers of King Street, St. James's, London, have held increasingly frequent numismatic sales while Sotheby's, their main rivals in the fine art field, hold occasional sales. In February, 1968, however, Sotheby's took the first step in expanding their numismatic interests by appointing D. J. Crowther to re-organise and develop their coins and medals department. By the time this book is published the first effects of this development should be felt in the numismatic world.

Other auctioneers who hold regular coin and medal sales, though on a more modest scale, are H. G. Hughes of Chelmsford, Essex, William H. Brown & Son of Grantham, Frank H. Fellows & Sons of Birmingham, Ireland's of Norwich, Henry Spencer & Sons of Retford, Morphet & Morphet of Harrogate and Wallis & Wallis of Lewes. Allen & Townshead of Dublin specialised in coin sales, but have recently discontinued them due to an apparent lack of demand or interest by Irish collectors.

Because of the comparative lack of restriction on the import and export of coins and medals and the absence of a government sales tax, London has developed in the past into the centre of the world numismatic market and many collections, large and small, have been sent there for disposal by auction. Although the recent Gold Coins Order may have a detrimental effect on this in the long run London is still pre-eminent in this field. Nevertheless serious competition is offered by a number of Continental auctioneers of international repute.

One of the foremost is Jacques Schulman of Amsterdam, where many famous Continental collections have come under the hammer since the beginning of the century. Switzerland can boast two organisations holding regular auctions. Münzen und Medaillen (Coins and Medals) of Basle are noted for their specialised sales of high-grade material. Hess-Leu conduct two big sales each year, in the spring and the autumn, in the Hotel Schweizerhof on the shores of Lake Lucerne, and these are always sure to draw a large cosmopolitan group of collectors and dealers. Sales of a somewhat different nature are those held periodically, under the auspices of the Austrian government, at the Dorotheum in Vienna. These sales vary greatly in the quantity and quality of the material vended. The same curious system is applied in Paris, where miscellaneous sales of this sort are held from time to time at the Hotel Drouot.

On the other side of the Atlantic the leading dealer and auctioneer is Hans Schulman, a member of the same family whose name is a household word in Continental numismatics. Periodic auctions are held by this firm at the Waldorf-Astoria in New York. The other principal auctioneer is Stack of New York. Occasional auctions are staged by other dealers, while Dunn's of Norfolk, Virginia, conduct regular postal auctions. The lots offered in a postal auction are advertised some time in advance of a certain date, either by means of a list mailed to regular clients or by a display page in one of the numismatic papers in America. These lists and advertisements contain a coupon enabling prospective purchasers to enter their bids in good time before the closing date.

There is an element of uncertainty in bidding by post, though many collectors do it regularly and seldom complain about it. The Bid Form contains space for the signature, name and address, total purchase limit and the bidder and details of special instructions regarding posting if required. There are also printed columns for the insertion of the desired lot number, with the maximum bid in each case. Unlike stamp auctions, coin sales very seldom attempt an estimate of the value of the lots which is such a help to philatelists in determining what sort of bid they will make. Numismatists on the other hand are more in the dark, so that a postal bid can well be a risky matter —either far too low or far too high. In the latter case, theoretically, if your maximum bid for a lot is, say £25, and the next highest bid to yours is £20, then you secure the lot for one stage above that sum, i.e. £21. If the auction is reliable this works out; but all too often one finds in postal bidding of this sort that one secures a lot at one's maximum figure.

The converse is also true, with 'book bids' at ordinary auctions, but there is nothing that can be done about it. One will often find that a lot has been knocked down to a bid which is only one stage higher than one's maximum. I myself have attended an auction and been bidding 'against the book' for a lot, eventually securing it after the book bidder's maximum had obviously been reached. Auctioneers usually publish a list of prices realised following each sale and send them on to interested clients, so that one can always check on the price fetched by any lot and compare it with one's bid.

The bidding in an auction is regulated by the auctioneer and, if there is no reserve price, it is left to his discretion to determine the starting price and the rate of the advances in the bidding.

As an alternative to bidding by post you can commission an agent on your behalf. Most of the dealers who regularly attend the auctions will bid for you and the small fee which they charge for doing so is well worth it. In fact, a useful piece of advice to the novice in regard to auctions is not to bid in person but leave it to an agent whose knowledge and experience of bidding tactics is far greater. A dealer's advice is particularly valuable in the case of coin auctions since, in the absence of any estimated value of lots printed in the auction catalogue, the would-be purchaser may have a very hazy idea as to the probable market value of the items he requires, whereas the dealer, who is in close touch with prevailing prices and is acutely aware of any fluctuations in the market, can usually form an accurate opinion of what a lot should fetch and bid for his client accordingly.

Whether you bid by post or through an agent it is extremely unwise to give the instruction to 'buy at best' or give an unlimited bid, even should the auctioneer or agent agree to do so. This places too much responsibility on them and, if they were to continue bidding on your behalf and eventually secure

PLATE IV

Foreign Coins

(1–7) France: Louis XVI, First Empire, Louis XVIII, Napoleon III, Third
Republic, 'Vichy France', Fifth Republic; (8–10) Germany: Empire, Federal
Republic, Democratic Republic; (11) Turkey; (12) Vatican; (13) Austria;
(14) Egypt; (15) Denmark; (16) Italy.

a lot regardless of the cost, you might be highly dissatisfied, not to say outraged, at the price you had to pay. Bert Seaby, reminiscing on forty years as a dealer, in the *Coin and Medal Bulletin* (July 1966) wrote:

'In December (1926) there was a small sale at Sotheby's that I shall never forget. It was a miscellaneous sale but contained seven American pieces that were illustrated. We received a cable from an American collector/dealer to "buy". I expected bids from an English collector so cabled back for further instructions and received a reply "buy against all opposition." The first lot was a Willow Tree sixpence which then, I suppose, was worth £30 at the most; I lost my nerve at £160 and let the auctioneer buy it at £165. The next lot was the rarest of the seven, a Willow Tree threepence; I bought it at £305 ($1,500) which was quite a crazy price at that time. The other lots were common Pine Tree shillings, then worth £10 each at most; they fetched £50 each and I did not buy any of them. This was a case where three of us had unlimited bids. I am pleased to say we were paid for the lot I bought, but we never did any further business with the buyer, who thought he had been the victim of sharp practice. I was in an unenviable position at the sale and should have been entirely justified if I had gone higher on the other lots. It taught me a lesson—never take an unlimited commission unless one is allowed to use one's own discretion.'

The anecdote sums up most succinctly the perplexing situation faced by agents with unlimited bids, so it is hardly surprising that they are most reluctant to accept them. There is a moral in this story for the client as well. He should be prepared to take the advice of his agent and fix a limit on his bid. The same holds good for the collector who bids in person, for it is only too easy to get carried away in the sale-room and pay far more for a coin than it is worth.

ADVERTISEMENTS

Another source of coins is the Advertisement section of certain newspapers and periodicals. In the United Kingdom the *Exchange and Mart*, published weekly, and *Hobbies*, published monthly, contain numerous advertisements from part-time dealers and collectors disposing of duplicates or unwanted material. A certain number of advertisements for coins and medals also appear in the personal columns of the quality Sunday newspapers, but the best advertisements are those which may be found in the numismatic magazines. Apart from the display advertisements inserted by dealers there are usually pages reserved for small advertisements in which collectors can publicise the material they have for disposal or, alternatively, the items they are looking for.

CHAPTER V

KNOWLEDGE PAYS OFF

THERE IS A story, probably not apocryphal, that the staff of a certain famous museum are in the habit of visiting a nearby coin dealer's shop, where they pore over the trays of assorted material priced from a few pence upwards and not infrequently chance upon an unconsidered rarity which goes promptly but unobtrusively to grace the cabinets of one of our great national collections.

There is no doubt that the true numismatist is the person who makes his hobby pay, profiting by his superior knowledge of his subject and enabling him to spot the rare and the unusual among the otherwise mediocre and mundane. Coin dealers, by virtue of the vast field covered by numismatics, can seldom be omniscient and many a specialist is able to take advantage of this and pick up items at a fraction of their true worth. Of course, as numismatic knowledge becomes more widely disseminated the opportunities of the shrewd numismatist will recede, though, conversely, unscrupulous dealers (a small minority, fortunately) will be less able to foist poor material at outrageous prices on to unsuspecting collectors. Knowledge is usually born of long experience and years of handling coins and the instinct (which does not grow overnight) for nosing out a good item.

In case I may be accused of being anti-dealer I must hasten to add that the best example I know of an expert numismatist recognising the true value of an item concerns the London dealer, Nick Parker, who had the following experience in 1966. He was one of a galaxy of international dealers who attended the most important gold coin auction in recent years. This was the sale of material from the Serooskerke hoard, auctioned by Jacques Schulman in Amsterdam and consisting of over a thousand lots of hammered gold coins spanning a period of two centuries (1422–1622). The hoard came to light during the redevelopment of a piece of land in the neighbourhood of the Serooskerke. During the summer prior to the commencement of the building project the ground was cultivated by the son of a local alderman and it was while he was pulling up a crop of leeks that a few gold pieces were unearthed.

The alderman, his son and a labourer began digging systematically and retrieved a few more coins and then excavation was organised by the local council. After a few coins had been set aside for the finders, the council and the Gemeente Serooskerke, the Royal Dutch Coin Cabinet picked out a few items and the rest were then sent to auction. About half of the find (which was evidently a scholar's collection rather than a miser's hoard) comprised Dutch gold, but most other European states were well represented.

Among the many fine English pieces was an angel of Philip and Mary (1554–8), described in the auction catalogue as 'rare and very fine', which was knocked down to Mr. Parker for D.fls 7,000 (about £700). Mr. Parker felt intuitively that this particular coin was not quite what it appeared and subsequent examination confirmed what a tremendous bargain he had secured. This angel has proved to be an official imitation, produced at a Continental mint, and is hitherto unrecorded. It contains gold of the correct weight for this denomination, but differs in several respects from the normal English type. The details of the ship on the reverse place it in a somewhat later period (i.e. Elizabethan). This coin is not comparable to Continental imitations of other reigns and, until a search of contemporary archives in Spain and the Netherlands can be made, the full story cannot be told. That it is exceptionally rare, possibly unique, there can be no doubt and its present value is thought to be nearer £5,000. The angel was the longest-lived and most widely used gold piece in late medieval coinage, popular not only in its native England but all over the Continent where it was recognised as a standard. It is not surprising that an official imitation should be produced; a modern analogy would be the Maria Theresa thalers dated 1780 which are still manufactured for circulation in the Middle East.

There are many dealers in Britain to-day who can claim a very profound knowledge in some specialised field and many of the staff employed by the leading firms, Seaby and Spink, have earned a wide reputation for scholarship. A good proportion of numismatic literature has been compiled by these men and women. Seaby's current publications, for example, range in scope from Frank Purvey's *Collecting Coins—for the beginner* to the recent first volume in a projected series dealing with Roman silver coins (Republic to Augustus). Spinks have tended towards more specialised publications, such as the excellent trio written by John S. Davenport and dealing respectively with European Crowns (1700–1800), German Talers (1700–1800) and European Crowns and German Talers since 1800. Howard Linecar of Spinks not only acts as Associate Editor of the popular monthly *Coins and Medals* but has written many books for the beginner and medium collector. Those members of the trade who have generously put their knowledge and experience at the disposal of the collector deserve not only to be congratulated but supported, for numismatic publications are seldom profitable ventures in the normal commercial sense. All too often, unfortunately, the numismatist economises on literature in order to have more money available for the purchase of coins or medals. Such a practice, however, is false economy. Foolhardy is the collector who would attempt to put together a worthwhile collection without acquainting himself as fully as possible with all the available knowledge on the subject. Twenty-seven centuries of coins produced in countless mints in every part of the globe amount to a formidable quantity of material for collection and study. It is accepted that a mere haphazard accumulation of pieces is of little value numismatically and thus the collector is forced at an early stage to specialise. This exercise is virtually impossible unless the groundwork for study is acquired, through reading the relevant literature. There are now comparatively few areas of numismatics which have not been written about, and in many fields the literature extant would fill a sizable library.

LIBRARIES

Apart from the general works and guides to beginners, numismatic literature tends to be either very expensive or out of print, so that it is not always possible for the aspiring numismatist to possess his own copies of the works he wishes to consult. It is very important therefore to have access to at least one good numismatic library. In the United Kingdom the foremost library is that of the British Museum. The general library is the country's principal copyright library and theoretically at least one copy of every book, pamphlet and periodical is housed there. Consequently, numismatic works published in Britain should automatically be listed in its general catalogues and be available to users of the Reading Room. A temporary ticket, valid for three days, may be obtained at short notice from the Director's Office. The general library also contains a reasonable coverage of foreign numismatic publications but is not so complete as the departmental library of the museum's Department of Coins and Medals. Access to this library, however, is restricted to the staff of that department and to *bona fide* students who should apply in writing to the Keeper of Coins and Medals in the first instance.

Excellent libraries are maintained by the Ashmolean Museum, Oxford, and the senior numismatic societies, the Royal and the British. In the latter case these libraries are accessible to members of the respective societies only. In the United States fine libraries have been assembled by many clubs, the best being those of the American Numismatic Society and the Collectors' Club of New York (the latter also catering to philatelists). Other important libraries in the English-speaking world belong to the Canadian Numismatic Society in Ottawa and the Royal Numismatic Society of New Zealand.

CATALOGUES AND HANDBOOKS

The essential tools which no collector should be without are the catalogues and handbooks relevant to his chosen field.

Numismatics is less fortunate than philately, in the comparative absence of priced catalogues covering the entire field. Such catalogues, where they exist, fall into two broad categories. On the one hand there are the general works which attempt to cover the world, usually the modern period from about 1800 to the present time. The other category consist of catalogues devoted to the coinage of a limited area, perhaps of one country or even one reign. Foremost in the first category is R. S. Yeoman's *Catalog of Modern World Coins* which contains comprehensive details of coins of every country arranged alphabetically. Broadly speaking, the coins from the middle of the nineteenth century are listed, though a logical starting date (such as 1837 for British coins) may vary this by twenty years either way. In order to compress the world's coins into one volume of 500 pages, however, the listings have to be in outline only. Thus the period of issue of a coin is denoted by first and last dates of issue (e.g. 1898–1911) and coinage during the intervening years may not necessarily be continuous. Different mint-marks are listed only in exceptional cases where their interest is considered important.

One price is given for each coin, in each instance for the commonest year and mint-mark, and at best the prices (in U.S. cents and dollars) are only approximate. With the rapid change in prices these days the prices quoted can only be regarded as giving a comparative guide to values, but this is better than nothing at all. This catalogue is published by Whitman of Racine, Wisconsin, who also produce *The Handbook of United States Coins* and *A Guide Book of United States Coins*; both of the latter books give comprehensive listings, with prices for American coins.

Other important catalogues which deal in general terms with a broad section of numismatics are those published by the Coin and Currency Institute, 134 West 32nd Street, New York. These are the monumental compilations of the Institute's indefatigable president, Robert Friedberg. Best known of these works is Friedberg's *Gold Coins of The World* which covers the gold coinage from A.D. 600 to 1958, and the *International Coin Catalog* which has run to several editions between 1949 and the present day. More recently Friedberg has produced *Coins of the British World*, attempting a guide to Commonwealth coinage from A.D. 500 to date. A very useful publication is *Appraising and Selling Your Coins*, known familiarly to collectors as the 'Green' book. It gives copious advice to those interested in the financial aspect of the hobby on such matters as care and condition of coins and their grading, but its listings are confined to the coins and currency of North America only (i.e. The United States, the erstwhile Confederate States, Canada, Newfoundland, etc.). Other works in the general category are W. D. Craig's *Coins of the World* 1750–1850, which is complementary to Yeoman's *Modern Coins*, and the two books by Wayte Raymond dealing respectively with coins of the world in the nineteenth and twentieth centuries. Here again some attempt at pricing is made, but the same qualification must be applied as in previously mentioned catalogues.

In a more particular category there are numerous handbooks and catalogues. Those that give some indication of value include Seaby's excellent publications, of which *The Standard Catalogue of British Coins* is the most important. This catalogue lists all the coins from the time of the Ancient Britons to the present. Those up to 1816 are priced according to type only, while those from 1816 onwards are priced according to each year and mint-mark. This handy pocket-sized book contains over 800 illustrations and lists over 4,750 different coins. For the convenience of collectors of modern coins only the period after 1816 is also published as a separate volume, while an abridged version of the catalogue (known as the *Concise Catalogue of English Coins*) is also produced, with main type listings throughout.

Among the other Seaby catalogues which assist the collector to determine the approximate value of his coins are *English Silver Coinage*, covering the period from 1649 onwards; the two-volume *British Copper Coins and their Values*, covering regal issues and tokens respectively: R. P. Mack's *Coinage of Ancient Britain* which lists 416 types of Celtic coins; *Roman Coins and their Values*, a general catalogue of 4,312 coins from 268 B.C. to 498 A.D. covering every denomination including gold; and the companion volume, *Greek Coins and their Values*.

Other catalogues which the collector will find useful in appraising the value of his coins are J. E. Charlton's *Catalogue of Canadian Coins, Tokens and Paper Money*; J. R. Croghan's *Canadian Cent Varieties* and *A Guide Book of Canadian Coins, Currency and Tokens*, by H. C. Taylor and Somer James. Apart from the books already mentioned American coins are dealt with in M. R. Craig's *Guide to the Grading of United States Coins*. Other parts of the world are covered specifically by Remick's *Australian Commonwealth Coinage Guide* and Alec Kaplan's *Catalogue of the Coins of South Africa*. For the Orientalist, E. Kann's *Illustrated Catalogue of Chinese Coins*, recently re-published in revised form, is of some value, in spite of the rather infantile American-English in which it is couched.

Of the catalogues which do *not* incorporate lists of values pride of place must go to the magnificent series published by the British Museum. The catalogues of the Greek Coins held by the Department of Coins and Medals now amount to 29 volumes. The Roman coins in the Museum are perhaps not so well documented, but the six-volume catalogue of the Imperial period (from Augustus to Pupienus) is surpassed in this field only by H. Cohen's *Medailles Impériales* in eight volumes. Apart from these monumental reference works there are many books of a more general nature. B. V. Head's *Guide to Principal Coins of the Greeks* is a good introduction to the subject, while *Historia Numorum* by the same author is still the standard work. C. M. Kraay's *Greek Coins*, with 20 colour plates and 1329 black and white photographs, is the most superbly illustrated book on the subject ever published. A very competent introduction to Greek coins is C. Seltman's book of the same name. For Roman coins the best general book is Harold Mattingly's *Roman Coins*, while the Byzantine period is dealt with comprehensively in H. Goodacre's *Coinage of the Byzantine Empire*. Hebrew coinage is covered by A. Reifenberg's *Ancient Jewish Coins* and A. N. Lahiri's *Corpus of Indo-Greek Coins* deals fully with an interesting period in the numismatics of the Middle East. For coinage of the Far East the various works of C. C. Vermeule and F. Schjoth are the most detailed yet published.

There are many works devoted to British coins, too numerous

to mention here. Apart from books which serve as an introduction to the subject as a whole, such as H. A. Grueber's *Handbook of the Coins of Great Britain and Ireland* and K. E. Bresset's *Guide Book of English Coins*, every facet of British coinage has been documented in detail. Pre-eminent in the base metal field is C. W. Peck's *English Copper, Tin and Bronze Coins* 1558–1958, while the books of E. Hawkins and R. Kenyon on the silver and gold coins of England respectively cover the precious metals. J. North's two volumes on the hammered coinage of England deal with the period from 650 to 1662. The most informative of modern works on Anglo-Saxon coinage is the *festschrift* for Sir Frank Stenton edited by R. H. M. Dolley. Mr. Dolley is also the author of two compact booklets published by the British Museum and introducing the layman to Anglo-Saxon pennies and coins of the Dane-law.

An important development in recent years has been the publication of a sylloge of coins of the British Isles, comprising catalogues of these coins in various museum collections. The works which have so far appeared are *Ancient British and Anglo-Saxon Coins* (Fitzwilliam Museum), *Anglo-Saxon Coins* and *The Coins of the Coritani* (Hunterian Museum), *Ancient British and Anglo-Saxon Coins before Aethelred II* and its sequel, *Anglo-Saxon Coins of Aethelred II* (National Museum, Copenhagen), *the Willoughby Gardner Collection of Chester Coins* (Grosvenor Museum) and *Hiberno-Norse Coins* (British Museum).

Relatively little has been written in book form about the numismatics of Scotland and Ireland; these gaps are filled to some extent by I. H. Stewart's *Scottish Coinage* and P. Nolan's *Monetary History of Ireland*. For the coins of the British Commonwealth the standard work is Capt. F. Pridmore's *magnum opus* in three volumes so far, covering Europe, Asia and the West Indies respectively. A general introduction to the subject, however, is provided by Howard Linecar's *British Commonwealth Coinage*. A specialised work on an interesting aspect of numismatics prior to the British occupation is H. C. Schembri's *Coins and Medals of the Knights of Malta* which has recently been reprinted.

The coinage of other countries is exceptionally well documented, though much of the literature on the subject is written in languages other than English. Below are listed some of the more important works, arranged by countries.

Australasia: *The Coins of British Oceania.* R. L. Clarke.

Austria: *Die Münzen Salzburgs.* G. Probszt.
Habsburg Coins 1780–1918. P. Jaeckel.
Austrian Coins 1918–1964. P. Jaeckel.

Belgium and the   *Catalogue of Belgian Coins,* 1832–1964.
Netherlands: *Nederlandse Munten van* 1795–1965. J. Schulman.
Les Monnaies des Pays-Bas Bourguignons Espanole. Gelder and Hoc.
Coins of the Dutch Overseas Territories, 1601–1948. C. Scholten.

China: *Chinese Currency.* F. Schjoth.
Coins in China's History. A. B. Coole.

Denmark: *Danske Mynter.* Mansfeld-Bullner.
Danmarks Myntwaesen og Mynter, 1241–1377. P. Hauberg.
Myntforhold og Udmyntinger i Danmark indtil 1146. P. Hauberg.
Danmarks og Norges Monter, 1541–1963. H. Hede.

France: *Atlas des Monnaies Gauloises.* H. de la Tour.
Monnaies Françaises. V. Guilloteau.
Monnaies Féodales de France. F. Poey D'Avant.
Monnaies Royales de France. H. Hoffmann.
Monnaies Capétiennes. A. Dieudonne.
Monnaies Carolingiennes. M. Prou.

Germany: *Germanic Coinages. Charlemagne–Wilhelm II.* W. D. Craig.
Die deutschen Reichsmünzen seit 1871. K. Jaeger.

Münzen der deutschen Kaiser u. Könige. H. P. Cappe.

Bracteates d'Allemagne. G. Schalumberger.

Deutsche Münzen der sachs. u. frank. Kaiserzeit. H. Dannenberg.

Münzwesen der Mark Brandenburgs. E. Bahrfeldt.

The Coinage of South Germany in the Thirteenth Century. D. M. Metcalf.

Hungary: *Siebenbürgische Münzen und Medaillen von* 1538 *bis zur Gegenwart.* A. Resch.

Corpus Nummorum Hungariae. L. Rethy.

Israel: *Israel's Money.* L. Kadman.

Italy: *Bibliografia numismatica delle Zecche italiane.* F. and E. Gnecchi.

Monete Italiane, 1796–1963. A. Pagani.

Refertorio generale delle monete coniate in Italia. G. Sambon.

Mon. dei Reali di Savoia. G. Sambon.

Mon. di Venezia. N. Papadopoli.

Corpus Numorum Italicorum. H. M. King of Italy.

Japan: *Japanese Coinage.* N. Jacobs and C. Vermeule.

Poland: *Handbuch der Polnischen Numismatik.* M. Gumowski.

Catalogue de la collection des medailles et monnaies Polonaises. E. Hutten-Czapski.

Portugal: *Precario das Moedas Portuguesas,* 1140–1960. P. B. Reis.

Descripcão moedas de Portugal. A. C. Teixeira de Aragao.

Russia: *Monnaies russes.* Baron de Chaudoir.

Catalogue des Monnaies Russes. V. I. Petrov.

The Silver Coinage of Imperial Russia, 1682–1917. H. M. Severin.
Gold and Platinum Coinage of Imperial Russia. H. M. Severin.
Coins of Kieff; Great Novgorod; Pskoff. Count J. Tolstoi.

Siam: *The Coinage of Siam.* R. Le May.

Spain: *Mon. hispano-cristianas.* A. Heis.
Survey of Medieval Iberian Coinage. J. F. Lhotka and P. K. Anderson.
Catalogo del Doblon de a dos Escudos. L. Lopez-Chavez and J. D. Yriarte.
Catalogo de los Reales de a Dos Espanoles. J. J. R. Lorente.
The Coinage of the Visigoths in Spain. G. C. Miles.
Catalogo de los Reales de a Ocho Espanoles. J. D. Yriarte.

Sweden: *Beskrifning ofver J. F. H. Oldenburgs Samling,* 10th–19th Century. J. F. H. Oldenburg.

Switzerland: *Münzgeschichte der Schweiz.* L. Coraggioni.
Die Taler der Schweiz. J. P. Divo.
Die Neueren Münzen der Schweiz und des Fürstentums Liechtenstein 1850–1963. J. P. Divo.
Catalogue of Swiss Coins. R. S. Poole.

Vatican (Papacy): *Catalogo delle monete pontificie.* O. Serafini.

Yugoslavia: *Corpus der mittelalterischen Münzen von Kroatien, Slavonien, Dalmatien und Bosnien.* I. Rengjeo.

PERIODICALS

It is not sufficient for the shrewd numismatist to study handbooks and catalogues in order to keep abreast of current developments. He must peruse the newspapers, magazines and journals in which so much of the latest research is published long before it gets into book form. For the collector who is acutely aware of the profit motive the graphs and tables indicating market trends from week to week are an indispensable feature of the 'popular' periodicals, while, at the other extreme a great deal of research work of paramount importance is printed in the proceedings and bulletins of numismatic societies and this may be the only form which it takes in print.

Thus it is not only advisable to study current periodicals, but to delve into back numbers and volumes of journals which have long ceased publication. Much in these dusty tomes may be of ephemeral interest only, or superseded by more recent discoveries; nevertheless a hard core remains which the serious numismatist cannot afford to overlook if he is to derive the maximum pleasure and profit from the hobby.

In the United Kingdom there are, at present, three independent periodicals, three house journals published by dealers and three journals produced by numismatic societies. In chronological order the first of these groups is the most recent since, apart from several abortive attempts by C. Hearn Nunn in the last decade of the nineteenth century, no commercial numismatic periodicals appeared until 1964. In that year Link House Publications Ltd., who had been conducting a popular coin feature in their monthly *Stamp Magazine*, decided to hive off the numismatic element in a separate quarterly entitled *Coins and Medals*. This was astonishingly successful, so much so that the following year the quarterly was transformed into a monthly and subsequently enlarged from octavo to quarto format. Originally edited by the Editor of *Stamp Magazine*, Arthur Blair, it has now been separated from its 'parent' and is edited by Miss Heather Salter, ably assisted by Howard Linecar. *Coins and Medals* is fairly general in scope, with informative articles covering the entire field of numismatics.

The success of *Coins and Medals* has tempted other publishers into the numismatic field. *Coin Monthly* is similar in content and also aims at the intelligent beginner and medium collector rather than the advanced numismatist (who would nevertheless find much of interest within the covers of both magazines). A radical approach in British numismatic publishing was provided by the appearance in 1967 of *Coins, Medals and Currency*, a weekly newspaper, a notable feature of which has been the striking use of colour illustrations. Coins and medals (being in gold, silver or bronze as a rule) do not lend themselves to bright colour effects, but this periodical also lays stress on bank-notes and paper money which (subject to certain Government regulations) can be reproduced most attractively in this way. As a weekly, *CM+C*, as it is popularly abbreviated, has the edge over its rivals and has already earned a wide reputation on both sides of the Atlantic for its crisp presentation of the latest developments in the more popular aspects of numismatics.

All three periodicals are pre-occupied to a certain extent with the financial side of the hobby—an attitude which seems distasteful to the more scholarly numismatist who may fear, with some justification, that this is an unhealthy trend. On the other hand, few of the 'old school' of numismatists can become so detached from the subject as to ignore monetary consideration altogether, and secretly many of them, if the truth were known, derive no little pleasure from watching the ever-upward surge of values as numismatic demand increases. There is no harm in the objective surveys conducted regularly by these periodicals, since they merely indicate in a clear-cut form the state of the market for the different coins (invariably British). *Coins, Medals and Currency* are not content to provide periodic listings of values on their own, but have also published comparative tables showing the state of the market at some date in the not-so-distant past. A slight element of danger, however, is inherent in the lists of the 'Top Ten' coins most likely to increase in value, published from time to time by *Coin Monthly*. If everyone took the tipster's advice and rushed out and bought these coins, an artificial shortage could be created which would undoubtedly force prices up temporarily, but might cause a slump in the long run.

Alastair Gibb, writing in *Coin Monthly*, brings a cool, analytical approach to the investment aspect of numismatics, whereas Patrick Finn, who conducts a regular feature in *Coins and Medals* adopts a more scholarly, objective style in assessing the trends of the market and pointing out fields which, at present neglected, might repay the student who is shrewd enough to investigate them at the right time. Because new issues of coins are infrequent compared with stamps and take up an infinite proportion of numismatics as a whole, they do not preoccupy collectors to the same, near-hysterical extent. Consequently, although there is a certain interest in market trends, the popular numismatic journals are free of the 'tipsters' who seem to be such a necessary evil in the equivalent philatelic press. Thus numismatists are mercifully spared the fatuous comments of the prophets who constantly trumpet their 'hot tips' and bargains, often to the detriment of modern philately.

The house journals of the leading numismatic dealers invariably derived from the practice of sending out lists of selected items to clients at regular intervals. Gradually these lists developed to include editorial matter and articles on various topics and thus came to have a permanent reference value. The premier publication in this field is *The Numismatic Circular* which was instituted by Spink & Son in 1893, and thus celebrates its 75th anniversary this year. It is still true to the concept of the original dealers' trade list since it is despatched by post to subscribers only. It appears eleven times a year and contains useful articles ranging from general to fairly specialised facets of the hobby, as well as the lists of material for sale.

From their commencement in 1926, B. A. Seaby Ltd. produced a weekly duplicated list. This developed gradually over the years, being type-set from 1936 onwards and, at the end of the Second World War, was altered in format and character to become the monthly *Coin and Medal Bulletin*. In many respects it is similar to *The Numismatic Circular*, with features of interest to the beginner and the specialist alike. Rather more general in character is *The Numismatic Gazette* published by Corbitt and Hunter of Newcastle upon Tyne. A complete set of the volumes of these three house organs would provide the numismatist not only with a valuable commentary on the changes in numismatic fashions and the trends in prices, both up and down, for all aspects of the subject, but with an astonishing range of numismatic information which is not to be found elsewhere. It is a sad fact that so much minor research

PLATE V

FOREIGN COINS

(1) Spain; (2) Bhutan; (3) Cameroons; (4) France; (5) Germany; (6) Ireland;
(7) Czechoslovakia; (8) Portuguese India; (9) Monaco; (10) South Africa;
(11) Liberia; (12) Italy.

work is published in such an ephemeral form only and for that reason it is often overlooked by later students. Perhaps because the commercial publications are of comparatively recent inception or because, by being commercial undertakings, they must cater to the widest possible readership, the standard of scholarship in them is more elementary than in the house journals which, 'preaching to the converted', can afford to adopt a rather more serious tone. At any rate it would be an act of extreme folly for the aspiring numismatist to ignore the house journals as being mere trade lists.

The most advanced numismatic publications, embodying the quintessence of research, are those produced by the three largest and most important numismatic societies in the United Kingdom. The senior society, the Royal, publishes *The Numismatic Chronicle* once a year, putting on permanent record the papers read before the Society, its transactions and work in the more advanced spheres of numismatics, with a strong bias towards the Greek and Roman series. It is issued free to Fellows of the Society, but may be purchased by non-members from the leading numismatic dealers. For the specialist in British numismatics, from the Celtic series to the present day, the bulk of serious research is published in *The British Numismatic Journal*, which contains the proceedings of the British Numismatic Society. It too is published annually and is normally available to members only, but can be purchased from numismatic dealers. A useful feature of both the leading society journals is the amount of space which they devote to thoughtful, reasoned reviews of books published in the course of the previous year. On a more elementary level, catering to the medium collector in particular, is the *News Letter* published by the London Numismatic Club.

Because numismatics are inextricably linked with history, archaeology and classical studies, a fair proportion of numismatic research is published in the proceedings and journals of bodies not wholly devoted to numismatics. Thus it is necessary to consult the publications of the Society of Antiquaries and county archaeological societies, for example: otherwise much useful information may be overlooked. This also holds good for foreign publications such as *Revue Archaeologique* (Paris) and *The American Journal of Archaeology* which frequently deal with matters (e.g. recent coin hoards) of numismatic importance.

There are several other annual publications which should be noted. Two of them are produced by the commercial monthly periodicals—the *Coins and Medals Annual* and *Coin Monthly Yearbook* respectively. Both of these are excellent value for money and contain useful features of reference interest. Looking through the 1968 editions of these annuals I note that *Coins and Medals Annual* contains a detailed and illustrated list of all the coins and government-issued medals released throughout the world in the previous year. The centre pages of *Coin Monthly Yearbook*, on the other hand, is devoted to a survey of the value of British coins from the farthing to the crown between 1816 and 1966. Both of them list the numismatic societies and the coin dealers of the British Isles.

The third annual is *Cunobelin*, the year-book of the British Association of Numismatic Societies. It lists all the clubs and societies affiliated to the Association and contains a number of papers of medium to advanced interest, but its most useful feature for numismatists in recent years has been the systematic listing of museums and libraries in the United Kingdom which possess coins, tokens or medals. Initially, this was confined to a general list of such museums but more recent yearbooks have contained descriptive articles about the collections, and even detailed inventories of the collections in some cases.

As one might expect, in view of the greater degree of numismatic activity there, North America can boast of a larger number of periodicals of all kinds devoted to the hobby. Unfortunately the quality of these periodicals is not commensurate with their quantity and there is no American equivalent of *The Numismatic Chronicle* or the *British Numismatic Journal*. *The Numismatist*, published by the American Numismatic Association (Phoenix, Arizona), is their elementary counterpart, containing features of general interest in the main. Slightly higher in academic standard is *The Canadian Numismatic Journal*, official organ of the Canadian Numismatic Society of Ottawa. The others are of general interest only but, in view of the large proportion of advertising which they carry, they are of interest to those who wish to analyse the American market. From a perusal of current American periodicals one gathers that indigenous coins, from Indian head and Lincoln cents to silver dollars, overwhelmingly dominate the scene, with various sets of commemorative medals (in particular, the various Presidential series) providing serious competition. Little interest is being shown as yet in European or British Commonwealth coinage—though what interest there is has already caused an alarming drain of material from Europe to America and one shudders to think what the situation will be like if the trans-Atlantic demand continues to rise. Interest in and articles published about, the Classical series are virtually non-existent, presumably since the Americans do not have such material so readily available to them as collectors on the Continent of Europe.

The following is a list of the commercial numismatic periodicals published in Canada and the United States:

Calcoin News. 935 Sutter Street, San Francisco, California.

Canadian Coin News. 62 Richmond Street, Toronto.

Coin Galleries Numismatic Review. 123 West 57th Street, New York.

Coin World. P.O. Box 150, Sidney, Ohio.

Colonial Newsletter. P.O. Box 2014, Little Rock, Arkansas.

Numismatic News. Iola, Wisconsin.

Numismatic Scrapbook Magazine. 7320 Milwaukee Ave., Chicago, Illinois.

Whitman Numismatic Journal. 1220 Mound Avenue, Racine, Wisconsin.

World Coins. P.O. Box 150, Sidney, Ohio.

These periodicals are all rather general in character with a very heavy bias towards modern American currency (including paper money) and commemorative medals.

Infinitely more sophisticated are the numismatic journals published on the continent of Europe. Many of them have been flourishing for a century or more and are veritable gold mines of information for the serious student. The premier journal, founded in 1836 and still going strong, is *Revue Numismatique Francoise*. Published in Paris by Société d'Editions les Belles Lettres, its emphasis lies in the Gallic and Frankish coins of France but it also has a bias towards the Classical series generally. Six years its junior, in terms of foundation, but equally scholarly, is *Revue de la Numismatique Belge* published by the Société Royale de Numismatique in Brussels and subsidised by the Ministry of National Education and Culture. The senior periodical in Italy is *Revista Italiane di Numismatica*, which has been in continuous publication since 1888. There is also *Italia Numismatica*, published in newspaper format at Casteldario (Mantua), but fairly advanced in scope in spite of its appearance.

From Eastern Europe comes *Wiadomosci Numizmatyczne*, published in Warsaw and catering mainly to students of medieval and modern Polish coinage, but containing a good measure of Greek and Roman studies as well.

There are also several excellent journals which have now unfortunately ceased publication. As they are to be found in most numismatic libraries I append a list of them below:

Journal International d'Archaeologie Numismatique (Athens 1898–1927)

Numismatische Zeitschrift (Vienna 1869–1933)

Numismatischer Verkehr (Dresden, then Halle 1902–1939)

Detailed lists of periodicals, past and present, are given in *Numismatic Literature*, a quarterly bulletin, published by the American Numismatic Society.

MUSEUM AND REFERENCE COLLECTIONS

In the quest for knowledge, reading about coins is beneficial, but it is no substitute for examining the real thing. It is important, therefore, to visit museums which have numismatic collections and make as good use of them as is permissible. I say permissible since, in view of the nature of the material, all museums impose restrictions, in varying degree, on students who wish to examine coins and medals. Some provincial museums in Britain, with a limited amount of material at their disposal, have made the most of what they have. Intelligent and imaginative use of display cabinets and frames, together with ancillary 'visual aids', help to draw the lay public towards numismatics. Displays in these museums are of particular interest and value when designed to show local coin finds. Even quite small borough museums have been known to excel in this field. Paradoxically, as regards the larger museums, it seems that the more material they have, the less is put on display. Thus one finds that the display of coins and tokens in Oswestry Borough Library is larger and more attractively presented than that in the British Museum.

Enough has already been written about the 'negation' of the collections in the British Museum, which rank among the largest and finest in the world, yet have barely a handful of Classical silver and some gold electrotypes on display in the adjoining Greek and Roman Life Room. The Museum's staff have been criticised for their seeming indifference to the general public and the numismatic proletariat. It is indeed unfortunate that a more comprehensive coverage of coins on display, to include modern as well as Classical pieces, could not be provided, but the Department of Coins and Medals, in common with many of the other departments (notably the Library) of the Museum, are at present, labouring under great difficulties, of which an acute shortage of necessary staff and accommodation are but two. The exhibition room of the Department was destroyed by bombing during the Second World War but, fortunately, the collections (removed to a place of safety) were unharmed. Since the war the offices of the Department have been rebuilt, including a fine Students' Room offering every facility to the serious student.

The Department of Coins and Medals has performed, and is performing, a valuable role in stimulating numismatic scholarship, not only in Britain but in the world as a whole. Intending

visitors should make a written application to the Keeper of
Coins and Medals, stating the reason for their visit and the purpose of their studies. The Students' Room is open from 10 a.m.
to 4.30 p.m. on weekdays.

The British Museum's collections of coins and medals are as
old as—nay older than—the Museum itself. The nucleus was
formed by the cabinets amassed by Sir Robert Cotton (1571–
1631) who expressed a wish that his valuable library of books,
prints, manuscripts and numismatic collections be utilised for
the benefit of the nation. His grandson, Sir John Cotton, the
third baronet, announced in 1700 his intention of giving the
Cottonian Library to the nation and, in fact, an Act of Parliament was passed that year signifying that Cotton was 'content
and willing that his mansion house and library should be kept
preserved . . . for public use and advantage' but he died in 1702
before this could take effect. Another Act, in 1707 declared
that the library and its contents should be purchased from the
fourth baronet for £4,500, but this was never implemented.
The ruinous state of Cotton House led to the removal of the
collection to Essex House in the Strand and thence to Ashburn-
ham House in Little Dean's Yard, Westminster, in 1730. After
many vicissitudes (including the destruction of much of the
library, though not the coins, by fire) the Cotton collections
were amalgamated in 1753 with those of Sir Hans Sloane who
died in that year and had bequeathed his collections to the
nation. In June 1753 the Act establishing the British Museum
was passed and subsequently the Cotton and Sloane collections
were transferred to Montague House in Bloomsbury, site of the
present Museum.

Coins and Medals formed part of the Antiquities Department
till 1861 when a separate department was established under the
keepership of William Vaux (who was also evidently one of the
earliest stamp-collectors). The original collections were strong
in Anglo-Saxon and English coinage and this emphasis was
deepened by the addition of the collection of English silver
pennies, formed by the Rev. William Southgate, in 1795. At the
turn of the century the Cracherode collection (rich in Roman
and English pieces) was bequeathed to the Museum. During

the early decades of the nineteenth century the Coin Room was greatly enriched by donations and bequests such as the accumulations of Miss Sarah Banks and her sister-in-law, Lady Dorothea Banks, the Townley collection of Roman 'large brass' and the judicious purchase of Samuel Tyssen's Ancient British and Saxon coins, and Barre Charles Roberts' English coins, the latter costing the Museum 4,000 guineas in 1810.

In 1823 the Royal Library of King George III was transferred to the Museum and its valuable collection of coins and medals added to the swelling numismatic accessions. Subsequent additions of importance have included the large general collection of R. Payne Knight, the Woodhouse, Thompson and Lloyd collections of Greek coins, the Wigan, de Salis and Duc de Blacas collections of Roman coins, the Evans and Graham collections of English coins, the Hawkins collection of English medals, the Freudenthal collection of copper coins, tokens and tickets of the world, and the Marsden, Cunningham, Elliott and Bleazley collections of Oriental coins and medals. Valuable acquisitions have come from such sources as the Bank of England and the India Office and important purchases, including the choicest items from the Trattle, Shepherd, Montagu and Lockett sales, have been made possible through the generosity of the National Art Collections fund and the Worshipful Company of Goldsmiths.

An important source of material for the British Museum is Treasure Trove. The Cuerdale (1840), Chancton (1866), Corbridge (1912), Chester (1950) and, more recently, the Newstead (1967) hoards are but a few of the outstanding finds which have enriched the Museum's collections. More on the subject of Treasure Trove will be said in Chapter XII.

The United Kingdom is fortunate in having several other great national numismatic collections of only slightly lesser a degree of importance. I have already alluded to Dr. Perne and Dr. Hunter who founded the collections housed respectively in the Fitzwilliam Museum in Cambridge and the Hunterian Museum in Glasgow. Both of these museums have had many subsequent accessions of material. Oxford has an equally comprehensive numismatic collection in the Heberden Room of the Ashmolean Museum. The National Museum of Wales, in Cardiff, and the Royal Scottish Museum in Edinburgh contain rather small collections, the former having a noticeable bias towards Welsh coinage from Roman times onwards, whereas the latter is general in nature.

The numismatist who would seek reference material of a more specialised Scottish nature would do well to visit the National Museum of Antiquities in Queen Street, Edinburgh. The Museum, which was founded by the Society of Antiquaries in 1780, has concentrated on the coins, medals and tokens of Scotland and has been fortunate in securing material from many of the coin hoards found in that country, augmented by material in recent years from the Cochran-Patrick and Lockett sales.

Several municipal museums in Britain can boast of fine collections. They include the Museums and Art Galleries of Birmingham, Bristol, Chelmsford, Chester, Glasgow, Gloucester, Nottingham and Preston. Even the smaller museums up and down the country can sometimes produce specialised collections of local interest, such as the extensive series of Buckinghamshire tokens held by the Aylesbury Museum and the display of coins of the Hereford Mint which is to be found in the Old House, Hereford. Many London boroughs have numismatic collections of note in their museums, while the City itself has some interesting material in the Guildhall Museum.

Most Continental capitals have at least one museum containing important numismatic collections. Many of them, such as the Cabinet des Médailles in Paris and the Kungl. Mynt Kabinettet in Stockholm, had their origins in the collections of the royal family and have subsequently become the property of the nation. There are many numismatic collections in American museums, ranging from the general assemblage of the Phila-Matic Center at Boys' Town, Nebraska, to the world-famous Chase-Manhatten Bank Museum in New York. The Smithsonian Institute in Washington is likely (at the time of writing this) to have its numismatic material subsequently augmented by the magnificent collection of gold coins formed by the late Josiah K. Lilly who died before a deed of bequest could be drawn up, so that special legislation is required to carry his wishes into effect.

In Asia India occupies a prominent place numismatically and there are several museums with collections of great importance. In particular the Indian Museum, Calcutta, the Punjab Museum and the Lucknow Museum should be noted, while Pakistan's leading numismatic collections are to be found in the Lahore Museum.

CHAPTER VI

COMMEMORATIVE MEDALS

A BRANCH OF numismatics which has generally been ne-glected, but which offers boundless possibilities to the dis-cerning collector, concerns medals. It is sometimes difficult to draw the line between coins and medals since many examples of the former may more properly be deemed as medals and were not intended primarily for circulation as currency.

In this category, for example, would be classed the splendid dekadrachms minted by Syracuse in commemoration of the victory over Athens in 412 B.C. (paralleled in more modern times by the victory of the American colonies over their mother country). The Syracusans commemorated their victory by holding games each year on the anniversary of the battle. The champions in the games were awarded ten-drachmae pieces which were specially minted for the occasion. These large, handsome silver pieces, with their profile of Arethusa on the obverse and quadriga on the reverse, featured trophies of arms in the exergue and it is thought that originally arms and armour were presented to the winners and that later these awards were commuted to cash payments. The coins were much larger than normal and were brilliantly executed by sculptors whose art has seldom been equalled in the 24 centuries which have elapsed since they were issued. It is open to question whether these large pieces were meant to circulate in the normal way and so they may be considered as the prototype of the commemorative medal.

During the Imperial period the Romans developed the coin–medal to a fine art. The cult of the individual during the reigns of Augustus and his successors had a marked effect on the development of portraiture on coins whose designs were subject to frequent changes and were strongly propagandist in nature. From coins of this sort developed the commemorative medals which flourished in the later part of the Imperial period. A thousand years passed, however, before the art of the medal was revived during the Renaissance. Appropriately, it was in Italy that medals were first revived by Vittore Pisano in the fifteenth century and developed in the ensuing two hundred years by Lysippus, Gambello and Pastorino in Italy, by Gebel and Hagenauer in Germany, by Dupré and Warin in France and by Thomas and Abraham Simon in England.

The medallic art went into eclipse in the seventeenth century, probably as the fashion for reproducing portraits in miniatures painted on ivory or vellum developed. Nevertheless, occasional medallists arose whose work was skilful and lively. In England the remarkable Wyon family produced many medals which are prized by the art connoisseur to this day. The sensitive portrait of the young Queen Victoria, on the obverse of William Wyon's Guildhall medal of 1838, remained popular throughout her long reign, being used for military medals and even postage stamps right down to the accession of King Edward VII in 1901. The sculpture of medals improved noticeably towards the end of the nineteenth century and has continued to rise in aesthetic appeal ever since. F. J. H. Ponscarme and J. C. Chaplain (France), Karl Goetz (Germany), Theodore Spicer-Simpson (England) and Anton Scharf (Austria) are but a few of the outstanding medallists working at the turn of the century and later, while at the present day, the highest traditions of medallic art are continued by Paul Vincze, the Hungarian-born sculptor now working in England.

The medals of the Renaissance period in Italy, France, Germany and the Netherlands were cast from moulds and it was not until the early decades of the seventeenth century that they came to be struck in the same way as coins. The reasons for this were partly the cost in making the necessary dies, for striking outweighed the advantages for a limited edition and, in addition, the much larger area and higher relief of medals made striking impracticable in many cases until the invention of the screw press made it much more accurate. Abraham

Simon made medals by casting, but his younger brother, Thomas (who worked with him and is thought to have put the finishing touches to medals cast by him), developed as a die-sinker, becoming chief engraver to the Mint and medal-maker to Cromwell during the Commonwealth. Although he is best-remembered nowadays for his exquisite 'Petition Crown', struck as a pattern after the Restoration, he was also responsible for some excellent medals, chief among which were those struck in commemoration of the Battle of Dunbar (1650) and the Dominion of the Seas (1665), both of which have considerable artistic merit.

The fine portrait medals of the Renaissance and later are of great importance to the art lover. In many cases only one or two medals were cast and the moulds then destroyed. Consequently they are generally regarded in a class by themselves, highly prized by the connoisseur and priced accordingly. At the other extreme, however, are the modern confections which caused such a scramble by 'collectors' a year or two ago. Undoubtedly, as has been mentioned in Chapter III, their apparent intrinsic value had a lot to do with their popularity, but it must be remembered that their actual gold content was only about 40% so that plain, honest sovereigns or ingots would have been a more secure form of investment. During their brief hey-day, however, prices *did* rise steeply so some people at least made a profit out of them. It must be admitted that they were produced frankly as collectors' pieces and yet many of them were aesthetically unsatisfactory; their long-term interest or value to the social historian was also negligible in many cases. This was—and still is—true of many of the commemorative medals produced in the United States.

These ephemeral gold medals should not be confused with those pieces, often in limited editions, struck for a specific event and fulfilling artistic criteria. Provided that the initial price asked for these pieces is not out of all proportion to their artistic or historic value, these medals are likely to prove a reasonable asset, rather than an investment. Medals marking contemporary events such as Paul Vincze's splendid Chichester medal or the recent Israeli victory medal are likely to prove more financially sound in the long run than any of those interminable and rather boring Presidential medals of the U.S.A.

Bearing in mind the event or person commemorated, the artistic merit of the medal itself and the technical competence of the medallist, one should be able to form an opinion as to which contemporary medals are worth collecting. Apart from contemporary medals, which are made for and sold to collectors (or are available in part to collectors) there are several other classes of medal, which may be worth considering. An important point to note about medals is that, apart from the very modern, 'commercially-inspired' medals, and those of earlier ages which had a great appeal to the art connoisseur, the other medals have been largely neglected and very little has been written about them. The door is wide open to the shrewd collector to cultivate this Cinderella of numismatics. Below are outlined some of the types of medal which offer plenty of opportunities to the discerning numismatist.

RELIGIOUS MEDALS

This category includes the amulets and 'touch-pieces' which were worn suspended from a chain or cord round the neck to ward off the plague, the 'evil-eye' or misfortune. These should not be confused with talismans which, like the Lee Penny of Lanark, were allegedly endowed with mystical powers. Touch-pieces in the strict sense were coins or small medals distributed at a special ceremony by the sovereign to people suffering from scrofula (King's Evil). Although the Emperor Vespasian is recorded by Suetonius and Tacitus as having healed the sick at Alexandria by his touch, the custom of royalty touching scrofula victims is thought to have been initiated by Clovis, King of the Franks (465–511), as a result of the conferment of this miraculous power following his baptism and conversion to Christianity in 496.

The earliest English monarch to touch for King's Evil was Edward the Confessor (1058) while the last ruler in Britain to do so was Queen Anne who performed the ceremony for the last time on 30th March, 1712, touching no fewer than 200 persons on that occasion, including the youthful Samuel Johnson. It is interesting to note that the pierced gold medalet which he received is now in the British Museum. Incidentally, Queen Anne's touch was of no avail in Dr. Johnson's case since he suffered from scrofula all his life.

At these ceremonies the sufferers were touched by the monarch who also hung gold medalets round their necks. In the late Middle Ages the gold Angel (a coin valued at a third of a pound) was popularly used for this purpose on account of its religious motif and inscriptions. The obverse depicted the Archangel Michael slaying a dragon while the reverse showed a cross in place of a mast. The Latin inscriptions ('By Thy cross, save us, O Christ, our Redeemer' or 'This is the Lord's doing and it is marvellous in our eyes') seem to indicate that, although these pieces were minted for circulation as coins, their other purpose was clearly recognised. Examples of these coins minted between 1470 and the reign of Charles I (1625–49) are found with a hole pierced in them; from a strictly numismatic point of view this may damn them in the eyes of some collectors, but makes them more desirable to others whose interests include touch-pieces. Charles II had special medalets struck for the purpose of touching for King's Evil. In many respects these gold pieces resembled the Angels of his predecessors but were minted ready-pierced and were never intended for use as currency. This gift of healing was one of the powers held by Divine Right by the Stuart monarchs and touch-pieces are also known for the Old and Young Pretenders (James VIII and III and Bonnie Prince Charlie) and the latter's brother, the Cardinal Duke of York (self-styled King Henry IX); conversely the Hanoverian kings felt that this healing power had not been passed to them, so touch-pieces do not exist for any of the Georges.

Touch-pieces of this sort are keenly sought after by specialists in this field but talismanic medals are generally neglected. They range from Oriental fertility medals worn by women to the more prosaic good luck charms used surreptitiously in Europe and America to this day. As a class they are not without interest for the light they shed on customs and superstitions, and they are certainly worthy of collection and study. A branch of this class consists of religious medals devoted to Christ, the Blessed

Virgin Mary and the saints, of whom St. Christopher, St. Anne and St. Anthony seem to be the most popular, though theoretically I suppose that at some time or other every saint in the calendar must have had a medal struck in his or her honour.

COMMEMORATIVE MEDALS

By far the largest class of medals are those designed to commemorate a specific event or person. No-one has ever attempted to list all the medals in this class but I would go so far as to suggest that they outnumber the coins which have been struck throughout the world, in modern times at least (from the fifteenth century onwards). Among the earliest are the medals cast in bronze in 1390 to celebrate the recovery of Padua by the Carrara family, the Council of Ferrara in 1438 and the French medals of 1449–61 commemorating the expulsion of the English at the end of the Hundred Years' War. Medals have been international in significance, such as those marking the centenary of the Reformation and produced in the Lutheran countries (Scandinavia, Germany and the Netherlands), or parochial, such as the bronze medal struck in 1873 to commemorate the foundation of Bolton Town Hall, inaugurated on 5th June of that year.

The number of medals is so immense, and the subject so generally neglected, that the intending collector would be wise to limit his interest to a comparatively narrow field. Thus one could devote a lifetime to the study of medals concerned with naval history—an examination of the comprehensive, though by no means complete, collection held by the National Maritime Museum at Greenwich will give some idea of the magnitude of this field.

If we take one isolated event in British naval history and study the medals struck in that connection, the magnitude of the problem becomes apparent. During the 'War of Jenkins' Ear' between Britain and Spain (1739–40) a certain Edward Vernon, Member of Parliament for Penryn, was a voluble critic of the apparent mismanagement of the campaign and claimed that, if he were given a squadron of six ships, he would capture Portobello, the Spanish headquarters in the Caribbean. He was

taken at his word and given command of an expedition, which
did capture Portobello, on 22nd November, 1739, with the loss
of only seven men. Overnight Vernon became a national hero
and countless medals were struck in his honour. They are to be
found in gold, silver, bronze or pewter and they take many
forms, invariably portraying the redoubtable Vernon (who was
subsequently appointed to flag rank) on the obverse, and
depicting his squadron bombarding the Spanish forts of
Portobello on the reverse. Incidentally, Admiral Vernon was
nicknamed 'Old Grog' on account of his habit of wearing
grogram trousers, and the beverage of rum diluted in water
(which he introduced in the Royal Navy) is known as 'grog' in
his memory to this day.

Vernon's subsequent naval career was anything but brilliant;
he failed in the Cartagena expedition of 1740 and five years
later, while in command at the Downs, he leaked official secrets
to the press, for which act he was struck off the flag list. These
failings and foibles did nothing to diminish his popularity, as
the number of public houses bearing his name testify, and the
many Vernon medals are a mute testimonial to the adulation
accorded him at the time of his great triumph.

The souvenirs range from supreme examples of medallic art
to cheap pinchbeck pieces bearing crude caricatures unworthy
of any aesthetic consideration; and yet they are all of some
interest and value. The very first medal which I ever acquired
was a bronze Vernon which I purchased off a Glasgow street
barrow for sixpence. At the time I was intrigued because the
date of the event commemorated (22nd November) differed by
only one day from my birthday. At the time I knew nothing of
the redoubtable sailor-politician, or of the obscure naval base
which gave its name to London's best-known thoroughfare (so
far as antique-collectors are concerned), but since then I have
always kept a look-out for related items.

*Notes and Queries** once commented sneeringly on these medals,
but since that was written they have become very much harder
to find and considerably more expensive than when I first
began looking for them fifteen years ago.

* 3rd Series, ii, 70.

PLATE VI

UNITED STATES COINS

(1) Columbian half-dollar; (2) Kennedy half-dollar; (3) Indian Head cent; (4) 2 cents; (5) Lincoln cent; (6–7) Liberty dime and half-dime; (8) Roosevelt dime; (9) 3 cents; (10) 5 cents (nickel); (11) Liberty quarter dollar; (12) Jefferson quarter dollar.

Other subjects which might be worth investigating are those connected with transport development (particularly the canals and railways), politics (both satirical and propaganda pieces and items commemorating particular politicians and events), buildings (churches, palaces, town halls etc.) and historic events (e.g. the Great Exhibition, 1851, or the Columbian Exposition, 1893). Medals struck in honour of famous scholars, statesmen and scientists form important classes. A recent article in *Coins and Medals* (March 1967) dealt with medals struck in connection with Sigmund Freud, while, at the time of writing, several medals are in the process of manufacture in honour of Dr. Christian Barnard, the heart-transplant surgeon.

CORONATION MEDALS

The practice in Britain of minting special medals to celebrate the coronation of the monarch dates from 1547 when a large, though not particularly well-executed piece was cast under the supervision of Henry Basse. It bears the word 'Lambhith' in the inscription, implying perhaps that it was cast at the Archbishop's Palace in Lambeth. The original medal, cast in gold, is extremely scarce, but copies in silver are also known, though by no means common. His immediate successors did not follow this practice, though medals commemorating the marriage of Mary Tudor and King Philip II of Spain were cast by the Milanese medallist, Jacopo da Trezzo. King James VI and I introduced the custom of distributing medals at his coronation, a small silver medalet being struck for this purpose in 1604. The king was curiously styled 'Caesar Augustus of Britain and Heir of the Caesars', though James abandoned his pretensions of imperial rank after the first session of Parliament and settled for the humbler style of King of Great Britain.

King Charles I's coronation medal was produced for the same purpose, but with frank political overtones. Its bellicose Latin motto on the reverse, 'until peace be restored on earth', and depiction of a mailed arm wielding a sword, was intended as propaganda for the king's scheme to aid his brother-in-law to recover the throne of Bohemia. After the Restoration, Charles II had medals struck in gold and silver by Thomas Simon for

general distribution to the crowds who witnessed the coronation, as Samuel Pepys records in his diary; *St. George's Day* 1661 :
'meddalls flung up and down by my Lord Cornwallis, of silver,
but I could not come by any.'

The official coronation medals of King Edward VII and
subsequent rulers have been mounted with suspenders and
ribbons and are intended for wear in the same manner as
military medals and decorations, but a great number of other
medals, both official and unofficial, are struck on these occasions.
Various corporations and civic authorities have struck special
coronation medals for distribution to worthy individuals and a
large variety of medals, in bronze, brass, pewter or aluminium,
have been struck for distribution to school-children as part of
the coronation celebrations up and down the country. It would
be impossible to assess the number of different medals which
were produced for the coronation of King George V in 1911,
for example. There are even unofficial coronation medals for
King Edward VIII who abdicated before he was crowned, and
although they commemorate a 'non-event' they are quite
highly prized by collectors of coronation souvenirs or Edward-
iana, apart from numismatics.

CIVIC MEDALS

This is an extremely large category since cities, boroughs and
towns seem to have been particularly fond of the medal as a
means of placing on record all manner of occasions of local as
well as national importance. A haphazard accumulation of such
medals could be formed at comparatively little cost, picked up
in junk shops and street markets, but such a collection would
have little value. A collection of medals connected with one
country, or even with one city or town would have more
purpose and meaning and consequently should have a greater
resale value than a sum total of the individual items. As well as
medals struck in commemoration of historic occasions, one
would include in this category mayoral and other badges of
office. These items are often interesting and ornate examples of
medallic craftsmanship, fashioned in gold or, more usually,
silver-gilt and inlaid with semi-precious stones or overlaid with

enamel in order to show the colours of the civic coat of arms. In many cases these badges are retained by the recipients after their period in office has terminated and eventually they come on to the market. They are relevant to a collection of medals connected with a specific area, while civic badges as such would form a collectable class in themselves.

PRIZE MEDALS

This is another very large class of medals, extending from the internationally coveted distinctions such as Nobel Prize medals and Olympic medals, to the humble bronze medal awarded to the runner-up in the chrysanthemum class of the parish flower show. Here again the field is so vast that the collector would be well advised to concentrate on a limited area. Sports medals can be sub-divided into awards made in connection with one particular sport (e.g. Football) or restricted even further (e.g. Cup-winners medals). The extent or limit of the collection is dictated by the availability of relevant material and by the size of the collector's purse; conversely the amount realised by such a collection when it is ultimately sold depends to a great extent on the degree of specialisation.

School medals are an interesting branch which might be worth exploring. They fall into two types—awards for scholastic or sporting attainments on the one hand and medals for good attendance. The latter were often meant to be worn by their proud recipients and may be found mounted with a ring or bar with brooch attachment for pinning to jersey or blazer. They were usually awarded for so many years perfect attendance and additional bars could subsequently be added for continued perfect attendance. Many of these school medals are quite competently executed and attractively designed, but to my mind the more interesting examples are those produced locally by parish school boards, often quite crudely fashioned and engraved by hand. These rather naive mementoes of otherwise forgotten 'general excellence' possess a curious appeal.

Prize medals cover many other aspects of human endeavour. Gold medals awarded by learned societies and institutions have an antiquarian value beyond their intrinsic worth, depending on the standing of the recipients. Thus the gold medal of the Royal Society awarded to Captain William Bligh of *Bounty* notoriety, for his services to botany and navigation, would fetch a large sum were it ever to come on the market. Medals of this sort, awarded to famous personalities, are either in museums already or are potential acquisitions of museums, so that the private collector invariably has a great deal of competition for such items. Conversely, the collector who possesses medals of antiquarian interest is assured of a good market for them, if and when he comes to sell them.

There are humbler categories of prize medal whose value to the collector may vary considerably. I know of collectors whose interests are confined to medals connected with horticultural exhibitions or shooting competitions. My own predilection is for medals awarded in philatelic exhibitions so that an interest in philately and numismatics is combined. This is a relatively new field since these exhibitions are less than a century old and few medals exist that were awarded before 1890.

PROPAGANDA AND SATIRICAL MEDALS

This group is much older than one might imagine, although as a medium of disseminating political ideas these medals received great impetus during the First World War. Great use of medals was made by the Cavaliers and the Roundheads during the Civil War. The Parliamentarians struck medals in 1642 to publicise their declaration defining their policy as 'the safety of the King's person, the defence of both Houses of Parliament and of those who have obeyed their orders and commands, and the preservation of the true Religion, Laws, Liberties and Peace of the Kingdom.' On one of these medals the King's portrait was even included, with an inscription to the effect that he should support the religion and freedom of his subjects by being advised by Parliament! The first major clash of arms between the Royalists and the Parliamentary forces was the indecisive battle of Edgehill, which both sides claimed as a victory and celebrated with medals accordingly. After the King's capture, trial and execution, memorial medals were struck by his adherents. An interesting example, of Dutch origin, depicts the head of Medusa the Gorgon and bears the inscription: 'They blaspheme God, they murder the King, they contemn the Law.'

The so-called Popish Plot of 1678 led to a spate of propaganda medals, many of which concerned the murder of Sir Edmund Berry Godfrey. It has been alleged that the Catholics planned to murder Godfrey in order to destroy evidence incriminating that arch-plotter, Titus Oates. Godfrey was apparently waylaid and strangled near the watergate at Somerset House and some days later, to avert suspicion, his body, transfixed by his own sword, was taken to Primrose Hill where it was dumped in a ditch. The truth of Godfrey's death has never been ascertained, and probably never will be, but contemporary political commentators had no doubt as to how he had met his end. Several medals exist which show the dastardly deed or portray Godfrey in the act of being strangled while at least one type shows the popular satirical device of reversible portraits of the Pope and the Devil with the slogan in Latin: 'The Church perverted shows the Devil's face.'

The often vicious politics of the eighteenth century also provoked medals for and against the opposing parties. John Wilkes was a favourite subject on anti-Government medals for his courageous, though often scurrilous, attacks on the Prime Minister, made through the pages of his periodical *The North Briton*. One of these medals shows a head mounted on a jack-boot (a pun on the Prime Minister, John, Earl of Bute) being attacked by an axe, with the inscription: 'Briton strike home.'

Continental medals aimed at projecting a political view-point include the pieces struck in 1572 to commemorate the massacre of St. Bartholomew when several thousand Huguenots were murdered in Paris in one of the worst outbreaks of religious violence in European history. A French medal, which sought to justify the act, bore the slogan 'Valour against Rebels.' The mass-murder of the French Protestants was also celebrated by medals struck in silver and gilded bronze in Rome. These medals, portraying Pope Gregory XIII on the obverse and showing the slaughter of the Huguenots on the reverse, have been re-issued in comparatively recent times as part of a series of papal medals. Medals were struck in England in 1793, in memory of King Louis XVI and Queen Marie Antoinette of France, following their deaths at the guillotine, in order to whip up sentiment against the revolutionaries.

Instances of propaganda medals being struck by the opponents of the cause for which they were originally minted are not unknown, illustrating the peculiar way in which propaganda occasionally boomerangs on its perpetrators. In anticipation of the invasion of England, the French produced a medal in 1804 depicting Hercules wrestling with Antaeus and inscribed prematurely '*Descente en Angleterre—Frappée à Londres* 1804' (Invasion of England—Struck at London, 1804). Since the invasion never took place, owing to the vigilance of the Royal Navy, the medal was never issued and its production was carefully hushed up. All that survives of this abortive issue is a unique proof in lead, and a few casts in sulphur. Subsequently, however, copies of the medal were made in England, no doubt in ridicule of Napoleon's bombastic project which came to naught. The imitations can easily be identified on account of the spelling mistake—'frappé' instead of 'frappée'.

But the best known case of this sort is probably the notorious *Lusitania* medal, cast in iron by K. Goetz in 1915, following the sinking of the Cunard liner by a German submarine, with the resultant loss of 1,198 passengers and crew. The origin of this medal has often been disputed, although the Germans have officially admitted to having produced it. As early as September 1916, for example, *Blatter für Münzfreunde* refers to it as 'one of the satirical medals cast by Karl Goetz at Munich, satirizing the levity of mind of the Cunard Line'—an allusion to the disregard paid by the Cunard office in New York to repeated warnings by the German ambassador, Count Bernstorff, that the *Lusitania* (which was carrying cargoes of war material to Britain) would be liable to attack. The obverse showed Death issuing tickets at the Cunard office, with the slogan '*Geschaft über Alles*' (Business above all), while the reverse depicted the sinking of a *Lusitania* shaped more like a battleship than a liner, and with her decks crammed with guns and ammunition. This medal was later imitated in England and copies demonstrating the ultimate in 'German frightfulness' were sold on behalf of a charity. The replicas are still quite plentiful in Britain and can be recognised as such by the British inability to get the spelling quite right: the month of the sinking is rendered as MAY instead of MAI, as in the German version.

* * * * *

From the foregoing it can be seen that the charm of medals lies in the story behind their issue. Because medals were produced as a reward for services rendered or for academic attainment, they have a personal element which coins usually lack. Because medals were produced in commemoration of a historic event or person, they possess a historical fascination which few coins can approach. Because medals are usually produced in a much larger size, in a higher relief than is practicable for coins, they are more capable of demonstrating the virtuosity of the medallist or engraver. These reasons should combine to make medal-collecting very attractive, but inexplicably comparatively little interest is shown as yet in this branch of numismatics, mainly on account of the paucity of literature on the subject. With every year that passes and the output of medals all over the world becomes more prolific, the likelihood of a comprehensive catalogue ever being published becomes more remote. Here, therefore, is a branch of numismatics which is wide open for further research which should enable the shrewd collector to profit in the long run.

Fine collections of medals exist in Britain's four major numismatic museums. In addition specialised collections are to be found in the National Maritime Museum (naval medals) and the Wallace Collection (Continental medals). Among the works which are invaluable to the collector are Leonard Forrer's eight-volume *Biographical Dictionary of Medallists*. This has, unfortunately, been out of print for many years but I understand that Howard Linecar is now engaged on an abridged version bringing it up-to-date. It is also significant that the amount of space devoted to medals in the various numismatic periodicals seems to be increasing.

The most important work for students of British medals is the two-volume *Medallic Illustrations of the History of Great Britain and Ireland* by A. W. Franks and A. H. Grueber, published between 1885 and 1911. It was preceded shortly by R. W. Cochran-Patrick's *Catalogue of the Medals of Scotland*. Maritime items are covered by two books written by the Marquess of Milford Haven—*British Naval Medals* (1912) and *Naval Medals of France, the Netherlands, Spain and Portugal* (1921).

Continental medals are discussed in Sir George Hill's *Medals of the Renaissance* (1920), but most of the catalogues and handbooks were published in the countries concerned. The most comprehensive include:

Delaroche, P. *Trésor de Numismatique et de Glyptique,* etc.

Domanig, Karl. *Die deutsche Medaille in kunst- und kulturhistorischer Hinsicht nach dem Bestande der Medaillensammlung des a.-h. Kaiserhauses.*

Mazerolle, F. *Les médailleurs francais du XVe siecle au milieu du XVIIe.*

Simonis, J. *L'Art du médailleur en Belgique.*

Van Loon, G. *Histoire métallique des VII Provinces des Pays-Bas,* and supplements.

CHAPTER VII

WAR MEDALS AND DECORATIONS

THE AWARD of decorations for military service is an ancient institution. In his *Antiquities of the Jews*, the historian, Josephus relates that, in the third century B.C., King Alexander was well pleased with Jonathan, the High Priest, and sent him a gold button as a mark of favour for his skill in leading the Jews in battle. Subsequently he was awarded another gold button for his distinguished conduct in the field. The award of jewels, gold buttons and badges for valour was carried on in most European countries on a sporadic basis but the present system of decorations and campaign medals is essentially a modern one, dating back no farther than the beginning of the nineteenth century.

Medals cast or struck either as awards for gallantry or for more general distribution to those who took part in a particular battle had their beginning, in England at least, in the sixteenth century. The forerunner of the modern campaign medals was the Armada Medal, cast in gold or silver, which appears to have been awarded to naval officers and distinguished persons after the abortive Spanish invasion of 1588. The obverse bears a flattering portrait of Queen Elizabeth (thought to have been designed by Nicholas Hilliard, the celebrated miniaturist) with a Latin inscription signifying 'enclosing the most precious treasure in the world' (i.e. the Queen herself). On the reverse the safety of the kingdom is represented by a bay tree growing on a little island, immune from the flashes of lightning which seem to strike it. This medal, and a similar type depicting the Ark floating calmly on a stormy sea, bore loops at the top so that a chain or cord could be passed through it for suspension from the neck of the recipient.

The Civil War produced a number of gallantry medals, the best known being the Forlorn Hope medal, awarded by King Charles I in 1643, and the Dunbar Medal of 1650. The latter, struck in silver, bronze and lead by Parliament in commemoration of Cromwell's miraculous victory over the Scots at Dunbar, is particularly interesting since this was the first medal to be granted to all the participants and not restricted to high-ranking officers or for individual acts of heroism.

Naval medals were struck in gold for award to admirals and captains during the First Dutch War (1650–3), and the Battle of Culloden (1746) was marked by a medal portraying the 'Butcher' Cumberland and granted to officers who took part in the defeat of the Jacobites.

Towards the end of the eighteenth century the vogue for military awards increased imperceptibly. A solitary medal, awarded to a Captain Ewing, for distinguished conduct at Bunker Hill (1776), was produced by the Americans during their War of Independence, though the Purple Heart—originally a patch of purple cloth sewn on to the uniform—was instituted during this period as a reward for bravery in action. The Siege of Gibraltar (1779–83) was marked by an issue of medals to the defenders, but this was of an unofficial nature, provided by the garrison commander, General Eliott, himself.

During the Napoleonic Wars medals were produced by Alexander Davison and Matthew Boulton and presented to officers and men who had fought at the respective battles of the Nile and Trafalgar. Mr. Davison also produced a Trafalgar medal in pewter surrounded by a copper rim; it is recorded that the seamen who received it were so disgusted at the base metal that they threw it into the sea!

At the same time, however, Government recognition was given to senior officers who had distinguished themselves in certain battles and engagements and a number of gold medals were awarded. The events thus signalised include the capture of Ceylon (1795–6), the Battles of Maida, Bagur and Palamos. In addition there were medals granted by the Honourable East

India Company to both European and native troops for campaigns in India. They are found in a variety of metals from gold for general officers to tin for the native sepoys. Towards the end of the Napoleonic Wars an Army Gold Medal was instituted in two sizes—large (generals) and small (field officers). Bars for second and third battles and campaigns were added to the medal, but when an officer became eligible for a third bar the medal was exchanged for a Gold Cross with the names of the four battles engraved on its arms. Bars for subsequent campaigns were then added to the cross (the Duke of Wellington receiving the Gold Cross with nine bars). A total of 163 crosses, 85 large and 599 small medals were awarded, so that, apart from their intrinsic value, these decorations command very high prices when they make a fleeting appearance in the saleroom.

Although the Army Gold Medal is known to have been awarded to eleven officers of the British and Spanish armies below field rank (i.e. major) and even to a warrant officer—Sgt. Major Don Santiago Ruiz—officers below the rank of major, as well as N.C.O.s and private soldiers were not eligible as a rule for any of these decorations.

The first medal awarded to all ranks of the Army was the Waterloo Medal, struck in 1815, to commemorate the decisive victory of the Allies over Napoleon. The medal was struck in silver, with a large steel ring for suspension by means of a crimson and blue ribbon. Several points governing the value of Waterloo Medals should be noted. In the first place the majority of the recipients substituted a silver bar or ring for the steel ring in order to make the medal more elegant in appearance. Although this was perfectly permissible and such altered medals are quite in order they are not so valuable to a collector as the original style (though the latter is intrinsically less valuable). Secondly, with the Waterloo Medal there arises a factor which largely governs the value placed on most medals since that date, namely, the recipient himself. In this case, it should be noted that medals awarded to General Colville's Division (2/35, 1/54, 2/59 and 1/91 Foot regiments) are not so highly regarded (and therefore not as valuable), on account of the fact that this Division was out on the right flank during the battle and took no part in the actual fighting.

No action was taken to grant medals for the other campaigns in the Napoleonic Wars until 1847 when Military and Naval General Service medals were awarded retrospectively to veterans who were still alive. Since applications were made, in some cases, in respect of campaigns more than fifty years earlier, it is hardly surprising that the number of medals awarded was comparatively small, while the number of bars awarded for certain engagements was quite minute. Some 25,650 applications were received in respect of the Military General Service Medal and 20,901 for its naval counterpart. No fewer than 29 bars were authorised for the Army medal, but a total of 231 bars was authorised for the naval medal—proof of the power and ubiquity of the Royal Navy 150 years ago. Paradoxically, multiples of bars are commoner for the military medal than the naval medal. Two soldiers received the former with fifteen bars and more than a dozen were awarded fourteen bars, whereas the record for the latter medal is seven bars (two recipients) while five men received six bars and fourteen got five. The number of possible combinations of bars with the Naval General Medal is infinitely greater.

The Military General Service Medal was restricted to land campaigns during the Peninsular War (1808–13), the American War (1812–14) and isolated actions in the West Indies, Egypt and Java, whereas the Naval Medal covered a far longer period, ranging from the capture of the French frigate *La Cléopatra* by *H.M.S. Nymphe* in June 1793, to the naval blockade of the Syrian coast in 1840, during the British operations against Mehemet Ali. Thus Naval Medals with the bar for Syria are relatively plentiful (7,057 were awarded) while in several cases bars were awarded to one man alone and in seven cases there were no claimants for bars at all. It should be borne in mind that applications for the medals and bars resulted mainly from the publicity given by printed advertisements and notices posted up all over the country. With the poor general standard of literacy prevalent at the time, many people who were entitled to the medals would have been quite unaware of their existence.

Particularly scarce are the bars awarded to the Naval General Service medal for 'Boat Service'. Altogether there were 55 bars of this type which were sanctioned for minor engagements involving ships' boats in which one or more officers were promoted as a result. The largest scale boat action was that which took place off New Orleans on 14th December, 1814, involving the destruction of the American guard-ships; this resulted in the award of 214 bars. The next most plentiful bars are those for Boat Service dated 1st November, 1809 (118), 23rd November, 1810 (65), and April and May, 1813 (55), while in five cases only one bar is known to have been awarded. Thus medals with any of these rare bars are highly prized indeed and fetch large sums. A Naval General Service Medal bearing three bars was sold at Sotheby's in February, 1968, for £600—a comparatively large sum, but understandable when one realises that two of the bars were extremely scarce. Of one, inscribed 'Emerald 13th March, 1808' only twelve were awarded and only ten of another, inscribed for Boat Service 4th June, 1805. Medals with more than one bar (other than the combination 'Navarino' and 'Syria') are none too common anyway but where a rare bar is present, either alone or in combination with another, the value of the medal can rise enormously.

The Naming of Medals

The Military and Naval General Service Medals, with their multitudinous combinations of bars, have long been popular with collectors, but the other campaign medals of the past 120 years have a strong following as well. With the exception of the stars and medals awarded during the Second World War, all British campaign medals have borne the name of the recipient and usually his (or her) number, regiment and rank as well. This brings a personal element into the study of medals which is lacking in most other branches of numismatics. The name on a medal is very important for two reasons. It is a means of testing the genuineness, not only of the medal itself, but its bar combination, and secondly it enables the collector to link the medal not only with the man who won it, but with his unit or formation, and thus plays a vital part in the development of naval or military history, if only a small part in most cases.

Much of the potential value of a medal depends on the man who won it, or the unit to which he belonged. Since it would be impossible to collect medals in a general fashion, the collector must specialise in some aspect of the subject, restricting his interests perhaps to one medal (e.g. British campaigns in India), or to medals and decorations awarded to the men of one regiment. The information given on the rim or back of a medal is therefore important in helping to identify it and assign it to its correct place. Even this has to be qualified to some extent. Some regiments are more popular than others with collectors and much depends on the part, active or passive, played by a unit in a particular battle or campaign for which the medal was awarded. Then again, the combination of event with the corps or regiment of the recipient must be considered.

At one extreme we find the Royal Regiment of Artillery, living up to its motto 'Ubique', by being represented in virtually every land action (and not a few naval actions, as witness the Atlantic Star worn by former Maritime Gunners still serving with the Regiment), so that a comprehensive collection of medals awarded to the R.A. would be a formidable feat. At the other extreme one finds odd detachments, sometimes consisting of one or two men only, seconded from a regiment for service with another unit. The Indian General Service Medal, with bar for Hazara 1891, is usually found named to personnel of the 11th Bengal Lancers and various battalions of the Bengal Infantry, but according to the medal rolls it was also given to six men of the 2nd Manchester Regiment, two men of the Queen's Regiment and one each to troopers of the 2nd and 7th Dragoon Guards. Whereas a specimen of the I.G.S. with this bar is not hard to find named to a soldier in one of the Bengal units, it constitutes a major rarity when awarded to one of the 'odd men' and its value is correspondingly high.

Since the personal details given on a medal regarding the recipient are so important, it is necessary for the collector to verify two facts—that the person whose name is on the medal was actually present at the action for which either the medal or its bars were awarded, and secondly, that the naming of the bar and the attachment of the bars is correct and not tampered with in any way. As regards the first, the Public Record Office in Chancery Lane, London, is a gold mine of information for all naval and military campaigns. Apart from despatches, reports and muster rolls covering the actions, there are the medal rolls compiled from the applications for medals and bars. Transcriptions of the medal rolls are held by regimental museums in many cases, and also by such bodies as the Military Historical Association. The rolls, while extremely useful, must be used with caution.

The presence of a name on the roll does not mean that a medal or bar was inevitably awarded; conversely authenticated medals are known to exist named to persons not listed on the medal roll. There are often divergences between the muster and medal rolls. Moreover discrepancies in the spelling of recipients' names are not uncommon and bars are sometimes found listed for regiments which were not even in existence when the battle was fought! This is explained, however, by the fact that a man may have been serving with one unit which took part in the campaign and subsequently transferred to another. When claiming his medal he probably gave his *present* unit, rather than the one in which he was serving at the time of the action.

Unfortunately cases of medals having been tampered with are by no means rare, so it is necessary to be able to recognise evidence of fakery. A favourite device of the faker is to alter the name and personal details of the recipient and to substitute another name in order to enhance the medal's value. This is done simply by filing the inscription off the rim and adding a new one. In order to check a medal for such alterations a similar medal of proven genuineness should be compared with the suspect and their diameters checked carefully with a pair of fine callipers. Take the measurements at several points round the rim so that any unevenness should soon be apparent.

I cannot stress too much the importance of being closely familiar with the various styles of naming medals. The naming of British campaign medals is fully dealt with in a series of articles by Alec A. Purves in *Coins and Medals* (November 1966–

April 1967). From this it will be seen that an incredible variety of lettering—roman, italic, script, sans-serif, seriffed in all shapes and sizes—has been used at one time or another. In some cases the inscription has been applied by impressing; in others the inscription is engraved by hand. If a medal is normally impressed and you come across an engraved example you should immediately be on your guard. This is not an infallible test, however, since medals have been known with more than one style of naming, particularly if duplicates were issued at a much later date to replace medals lost or destroyed.

A rather more subtle approach was adopted by some fakers in respect of the Naval General Service Medal. The three commonest bars Algiers (1,362), Navarino (1,137) and Syria (7,057) were awarded to many recipients possessing common names such as Jones or Smith which can be matched with recipients of some very rare bars. In the case of the N.G.S. the ship on which the recipient served is not given, thus aiding the fraudulent substitution of bars. It is necessary therefore to check the condition of the bars, even if the naming appears to be correct. Points to watch for are file or solder marks on the rivets which secure the bars to each other and to the suspender of the medal. This test is not infallible since bars *do* occasionally work loose if subject to constant wear (particularly if the recipient was a cavalryman, for obvious reasons). But bars whose rivets appear to have been hammered should automatically be suspect, until a check of the medal roll passes them as authentic. Examples of the earlier medals, particularly those awarded to officers, may be found with unorthodox coupling of bars. Major L. L. Gordon, in his definitive work *British Battles and Medals*, mentions a Naval General Service Medal awarded to one of his ancestors, with bars for Guadaloupe and Anse la Barque in a large rectangular style which must have been quite unofficial. The medal is quite authentic, so it must be presumed that officers were allowed a certain degree of latitude in the manner in which they altered their medals.

With the collector of British campaign medals the person to whom the medal was awarded becomes almost as important as the medal itself. It is not sufficient to collect the medal and leave

PLATE VII
CROWN PIECES

1) Panama balboa; (2) Britain 'Jubilee' crown; (3) New Zealand dollar; (4) Zambia crown; (5) Sharjah 'Kennedy' 5 rupees; (6) Tonga 2 pa'angas.

it at that. The collector must investigate it and delve into the archives to find out all that he can about the recipient. This can be a fascinating pastime and the value of the medal is greatly enhanced when the background to the award and the story of the man who won it is ascertained. The Public Record Office and regimental museums have already been mentioned as a useful source of information, apart from the muster and medal rolls which only provide the bare details of the award.

If we take the case of that rare N.G.S. which fetched £600 at Sotheby's we find it listed in the auction catalogue as follows:

> Lot 350 Naval General Service medal, 1793–1840, three bars, 4 June Boat Service, 1805, Emerald 13 March 1808, Basque Roads 1809, Edward Saurin, Lieut. R.N., *almost extremely fine and extremely rare.*
>
> **** 4th June, 1805 (Mid. 'Loire'), ten bars awarded; Emerald, 13th March, 1808 (Lieut.) twelve bars issued; Basque Roads, 1809 (Lieut. 'Emerald'). For further details see O'Byrne, p. 1031.

'O'Byrne' is the name by which the *Naval Biographical Dictionary* compiled by William O'Byrne is familiarly known to naval historians. This encyclopaedic work, published in two volumes in 1849, was contemporaneous with the authorisation of the N.G.S. and is a most useful reference book, since it contains detailed biographies of officers of the Royal Navy, of the rank of lieutenant and above. The biographical details of Edward Saurin, for example, occupy almost a whole column and from them we learn that he was the son of the Right Honourable William Saurin, Attorney-General for Ireland. He entered the Navy in August 1803 as a Volunteer, on board the 36 gun *Euryalus* and served on the Irish station. In May 1804 he joined *H.M.S. Loire* where he served as a Midshipman. O'Byrne states:

'He was under fire, during that period, of the batteries in Muros Bay, when they were gallantly stormed and carried, and the privateers *Confiance* and *Belier* taken, by the boats under the late Sir Jas. Lucas Yeo, 4 June, 1805.'

This gives the explanation for his Boat Service bar. O'Byrne then states that Saurin served in *H.M.S. Emerald* under Captain F. L. Maitland, rising in rank from Midshipman to Master's Mate and then to Lieutenant in 1810. O'Byrne continues:

'. . . contributed, on the night of 13 March, 1808, to the destruction in Vivero Harbour, of a large French schooner, *L'Apropos*, of 8 guns and 70 men;'
To this is added a footnote:

'On this occasion he landed with a party under Lieut. Chas. Bertram, assisted in taking possession of a battery (whose guns, 8 24-pounders, were at the same time spiked) and, after having encountered and routed the crew, was for several hours engaged (under the annihilating fire of a body of troops not 30 yards distant) in a fruitless attempt to launch the schooner, which had been run on the rocks, and was in consequence set fire to and blown up.'

Details of this exploit were also given in *The London Gazette* (1808, p. 416) while an interesting despatch from Captain Maitland to Admiral Lord Gardner, written the following day, gives a most vivid account of this spirited action and is published in full under the entry for Maitland in John Marshall's *Royal Naval Bibliography*, published in 1824. The latter work only deals with officers of the rank of commander and above, but the despatch referred to mentions Mr. Saurin as a Master's Mate. By inference we learn that Saurin was not wounded on this occasion, though casualties were very heavy. Conversely, during an attack on the island of Lissa in May 1812, he was severely wounded. O'Byrne says that he lost his right arm, his left was shot through, his neckcloth was cut through the different folds and his sabre was broken by a ball. This boat action, in which 20 men serving under Saurin were killed, did not warrant the authorisation of a bar although it seemed to have fulfilled the requirements for this, since Saurin was promoted to Commander on the strength of it. His third bar was, in fact, gained as a Lieutenant aboard the *Emerald* in April 1809 when she was one of several ships present at the destruction of the French fleet in the Basque Roads. Subsequently Saurin was promoted to Captain in June 1814, but never served in an active capacity in this rank, remaining on half pay, with a pension of £300 per annum, till he 'retired' in October 1846. He held the appointment of Commissioner of Stamps and Taxes for many years and, in July 1828, married Lady Mary Ryder, second daughter of the Earl of Harrowby. From the *Dictionary of National Biography* we glean the additional information that 'Admiral Edward Saurin died 28th February 1878, leaving a son, William Granville Saurin.'

Apart from the works of O'Byrne and Marshall, the earlier and later periods are respectively covered by Charnock's *Biographia Navalis* (published in three volumes between 1794 and 1798) and Clowes' *Royal Navy*.

The Army is not nearly so well served. Fortescue's 13-volume *History of the British Army* covers the period from 1660 to 1870 in some detail, but without the extensive biographical notes which distinguish the naval histories listed above. The gap is, however, filled to some extent by regimental histories and records, many of which have been published. Apart from medal and muster rolls most regimental museums will be found to contain documentary material, despatches, reports and diaries, relating to the actions in which the regiment has taken part, together with personal data concerning individual officers and men. There is no short cut to filling in the details of the personal history of the recipient of a medal or bar, but there can be no doubt that such background material adds greatly to the interest—and value—of the item. Ancillary material, such as photographs or portraits of the recipient or militaria directly associated to him, should not be overlooked. The converse is also true: an acquaintance of mine possesses a painting of a certain naval Captain, together with the sword awarded to him by Lloyds; it only remains for him to track down the N.G.S. awarded to the Captain and for this item he is prepared to pay handsomely!

MEDAL GROUPS

Apart from the combination of bars on a medal and the significance of the recipient, there is a third factor to be considered in assessing the value of medals, namely the relationship of one medal to another in a group awarded to one person. Just as, in the case of some of the medals discussed above, the number of bars on a medal is not in itself a significant factor, so also the number of medals in a group is not necessarily important *per se*. Groups of five or more medals, whose recipient can be identified, are by no means uncommon—for example, a fairly common five medal group would consist of: 1914–15 Medal, War Medal and Victory Medal (for the First World War) and the Defence Medal and War Medal (for the Second World War). Thousands of men served throughout the first war and survived to do duty, in a less active role, during a part at least of the second, long enough to qualify for the latter pair of medals.

It should be noted that none of the medals awarded for service in the Second World War was named to the recipient, so that groups comprising such medals alone cannot be readily identified and are thus lacking in the interest possessed by those containing named medals. Six-medal groups for service in the Second World War are not uncommon, particularly the combination of 1939–45 Star, Africa Star, Italy Star, France and Germany Star, Defence Medal and War Medal which was awarded to Army personnel who served from any time up to late 1942 and took part in the campaigns in North Africa and Europe. Conversely it would be possible for troops to have served over a longer period and seen more action, and only been awarded the 1939–45 Star, Burma Star (with Pacific bar) and the War Medal. Naval groups consisting of the 1939–45 Star, Atlantic Star (with bar for France and Germany), Italy Star and War Medal are less common and therefore more desirable (with, of course, the rider that it must be possible to identify the recipient), while the most desirable of all is the three-medal group of 1939–45 Star (with Battle of Britain bar), Air Crew Europe Star (with bar for France and Germany) and the War Medal. Such a group together with a Distinguished Flying Cross awarded to one of the 'few' is a highly coveted set indeed, providing, as always, that one can prove its authenticity.

I have illustrated a rather attractive group of seven medals which span a period of twenty years in the service of a soldier and illustrate the progress of his military career and the areas in which he fought. Yet one cannot get the whole story from the medals alone. 'They also serve who only stand and wait' is particularly true of the modern Army, many of whose officers have reached field rank without hearing a shot fired in anger and without receiving a single medal after more than twenty years service. The medals shown on Plate VIII were awarded to James D. Mackay (no relation of the author) who ran away from home at the age of fifteen to enlist in the Seaforth Highlanders in Edinburgh in 1880. During seventeen years of peace-time soldiering spent in Britain and Ireland he had advanced steadily in rank from private to sergeant-major, when his battalion was posted to Egypt. He took part in the campaign of 1898 to reconquer the Sudan and fought with distinction at the battle of Omdurman for which he was subsequently commissioned in the Dublin Fusiliers. His first taste of service in Africa brought him the Queen's Sudan Medal and the Khedive's Medal, the latter with the bars for The Atbara and Khartoum (a fairly common combination).

A short time later he transferred to the Middlesex Regiment where he was promoted Lieutenant and returned to Africa, this time on secondment to the recently formed King's African Rifles, with whom he served intermittently up to the outbreak of the First World War. His service in this area earned him the African General Service Medal with four bars. The first of these, inscribed 'Jubaland' was awarded for service against the Ogaden Somalis in November 1900–April 1901. The campaign in Uganda in 1905 brought him the bar for 'East Africa 1905'. By now he had returned to the Seaforths as a captain and was seconded to the K.A.R. for service in the Nandi country, recognised by the bar 'Nandi 1905–6'. The fourth bar, 'Somaliland 1908–10' was awarded for further services in that area against the forces of the Mad Mullah. During the Edwardian period Mackay served in Zanzibar where he organised the constabulary and taught the Sultan to drive a motor-car! This service was recognised by the conferment upon him of the Star of Zanzibar.

By the outbreak of the First World War he had been promoted to major and was again detached from his regiment to command native troops, against the forces of von Lettow-Vorbeck, in German East Africa (Tanganyika). In 1915 he was promoted lieutenant-colonel and subsequently was awarded the Distinguished Service Order and was Mentioned in Dispatches (as indicated by the oak leaves on the Victory Medal). Service during the war brought him the conventional trio of the 1914–15 Medal, War Medal and Victory Medal, which complete this interesting group.

While campaign medals are the category which the collector is most likely to come across, there are other classes which are not without interest. One group comprises the various medals awarded during the past 110 years for services on expeditions to the polar regions. The earliest of these awards was the Arctic Medal instituted in 1857 and covering service in voyages of exploration to the Arctic between 1818 and 1855. This medal is unusual on account of its octagonal shape, a format which is also characteristic of the subsequent Polar Medals. A second medal (circular in shape) was awarded for Arctic exploration in 1875–6, and a third, the Polar Medal, was instituted in 1904. The latter medal has been in use ever since, with only a change in the sovereign's effigy on the obverse. Incidentally, the original Polar Medal was designed by E. G. Gillick, whose wife, the late Mary Gillick, O.B.E., designed the profile of Queen Elizabeth currently in use—a unique example of a medal designed by husband and wife (though working fifty years apart!).

The first Arctic Medal is comparatively common, while the Polar Medal is, in most cases, extremely rare. It has been estimated that awards for service in the Arctic and Antarctic since the beginning of this century amount to fewer than a thousand altogether and when it is realised that over 90 different bars have been authorised, it will be seen that the Polar Medal is, in fact, an extremely rare item. The commonest award is the medal with bar 'Antarctic 1910–13' for Scott's last expedition, 50 medals and 63 bars being awarded. In many cases in recent years only one or two bars of a particular date have been awarded. Prior to 1933 the medals were either silver or bronze (in many instances the latter is actually a rarer award) but after that date all Polar Medals have been struck in silver. Additional bars are correspondingly scarce, the record being the silver medal with four bars won by Commander Frank Wild, who commanded the *Quest* on Shackleton's last voyage.

Another excessively rare category consist of medals awarded to Navy, Army and R.A.F. personnel for marksmanship. The Naval Good Shooting Medal, awarded annually between 1903 and 1914 for skill in gunnery, is comparatively common, 974 medals and 62 bars being awarded altogether. I use the word 'common' in a relative sense only since fewer than a thousand awards hardly makes it commonplace. But the Army Best Shot Medals are infinitely rarer, since usually only one of each class was awarded annually. The award of these medals was in abeyance between 1883 and 1923 when it was revived. Separate classes exist for the Regular and Territorial forces, and Commonwealth units. A more recent medal is the Queen's Medal for Champion Shots of the Air Forces, instituted in 1953.

Long Service and Good Conduct Medals do not appear to excite the same interest among collectors as campaign awards. Perhaps this may be accounted for by their 'image' of stolid devotion to duty rather than the romantic connotations of a medal with an unusual bar awarded for service in some remote and all but forgotten outpost of the Empire.

Service medals include not only such well known types as the Army L.S.G.C. (known affectionately as 'the mark of the beast' on account of its high incidence on the chests of sergeant-majors), but also awards to the Territorial and Reserve forces, the auxiliary forces, the Nursing Services, and organisations such as the Royal Observer Corps and the Cadet Force, the Police, the Red Cross and St. John Ambulance Brigade. The Special Constabulary and Fire Brigades also have their own medals bestowed according to length of service and distinguished conduct. They may lack the glamour of naval and military awards, but some day they may become fashionable with collectors.

DECORATIONS

Awards for individual acts of heroism and decorations for distinguished military, political or social service fall into another category altogether. Here again, collectors undoubtedly prefer a decoration awarded for bravery in the field rather than a political honour given automatically to a Civil Servant, just because he happens to have been in a particular grade for a certain number of years. The debasement of civil awards such as the M.B.E. is reflected in the relative lack of interest shown by collectors; although the tendency in the past year or two, to cut down the spate of awards in the half-yearly Honours Lists, may help to redress the balance in the long run.

It is generally true to say that military decorations are more desirable, but it is important to note that one decoration may be more highly prized than another, while the same decoration may be more valuable to collectors when issued in one period than in another. At one extreme is the greatly coveted Victoria Cross, only 1,036 of which have been awarded since its inception in 1856 during the Crimean War. At the other extreme is the Military Medal, instituted in 1916 for award to N.C.O.s and private soldiers; no fewer than 115,589 were awarded during the First World War. For this reason a M.M. from this period can be picked up for a pound or two, whereas one awarded during the Second World War can cost more than ten times that amount on account of its comparative rarity. Military Medals awarded for bravery in Korea and more recent campaigns are even more highly regarded, partly on account of the fact that relatively few were awarded, and partly because they are for the most part still in the proud possession of the original recipients.

Even the Victoria Cross itself can vary greatly in value. In 1920 prices varied between £75 and £150; forty years later the average price had risen to £500, while now prices range from about £750 to more than twice that sum. Generally speaking, V.C.s won in the Crimean War (111 awarded) are less highly regarded than Crosses awarded during the First World War, where, although numerically greater (633), they were far more dearly won. Second World War crosses are correspondingly more expensive since only 182 were awarded and comparatively few of them have so far come on the market. Incidentally, an identical number of V.C.s was awarded during the Indian Mutiny (1856–7) alone! Only five V.C.s have been awarded since 1945: to Lieut.-Colonel Carne, Major Muir, Lieut. Curtis and Private Speakman in Korea, and to Rambahadur Limbu in North Borneo. None of these Crosses has come on the market or is likely to do so for a very long time. V.C.s may not be disposed of during the life-time of the holder.

Certain other factors have to be taken into consideration in assessing the value of a Victoria Cross. The defence of Rorke's Drift was almost the only boost to British morale in an otherwise disastrous campaign whose nadir was reached with the annihilation of the British Army by the Zulus at Isandhlwana in 1879. The victorious Zulus moved on the Drift, but were met by the spirited resistance of the 139-man garrison of the 24th regiment (South Wales Borderers). The Borderers sustained 17 dead and ten wounded, although the Zulus left more than 350 dead on the battlefield. The engagement lasted throughout the night and eleven of the defenders won the Victoria Cross before breakfast. The value of Rorke's Drift Crosses, at one time not particularly highly regarded, has shot up dramatically in the past year or two as a result of the publicity accruing from the epic film *Zulu* which was based on this action. As a result, a Rorke's Drift Cross would now fetch over £1,000—ten times the price paid for the V.C. awarded to Private William Jones when it came up at Glendining's in June 1917. Incidentally there is also a great demand at the moment for the Zulu War Medal, particularly if named to a soldier in the 24th Foot.

Decorations awarded to officers tend to fetch more than those awarded to other ranks, mainly because they are proportionately rarer but also because it is usually easier to trace the personal details of an officer. The rank of the recipient may have some bearing on the demand for a particular decoration.

Military Crosses awarded to warrant officers are scarcer than those awarded to subalterns and captains.

Distinguished Service Orders could be won by commissioned officers of any rank but after 1914, when the Military Cross was instituted, it was usually restricted to officers of field rank. D.S.O.s awarded to lieutenants and captains in the Army in both World Wars are therefore very rare and invariably expensive, since they were awarded for acts of heroism which in earlier campaigns might have merited the V.C. The branch of the Services is an important factor also; the D.S.O. awarded in the Second World War is comparatively scarce to officers of the Royal Navy and much more plentiful to officers of the Royal Air Force. The opportunity for individual acts of bravery presented itself less often to sailors in the Second World War than to air crew; thus peculiarly naval awards, such as the Conspicuous Gallantry Medal and the Distinguished Service Cross, are much more scarce than the corresponding R.A.F. awards, the Distinguished Flying Cross and Medal.

The addition of bars to gallantry decorations greatly enhances the scarcity and value of these medals. The V.C., for example, has been won by three men on two occasions; so far as I am aware none of these V.C. and bar combinations has ever come on the market. An average M.M. from the First World War would be worth from £2 to £4 today, but with the addition of a bar for a subsequent award its value would jump immediately to about £10–£15, while M.M.s with two or more bars are very much more expensive.

It is important to note that in some cases (the D.S.O., for example) decorations were issued unnamed. For this reason the citation or other documents relevant to the award should be kept with the decoration wherever possible.

ORDERS OF CHIVALRY

British orders range in antiquity from the medieval Orders of the Garter and the Bath to the Order of the British Empire instituted during the First World War. They are interesting and colourful in many cases, with breast stars, collars, chains and garters, but relatively few of these richly jewelled decorations ever come on the market since most of them do not belong to their wearers and have to be returned to the Central Chancery of Knighthood following the death of their recipients. Similar regulations concern many foreign orders of chivalry and many collectors will recall the trouble and embarrassment caused ten years ago when the Egyptian Government tried to auction the orders and decorations left behind by King Farouk. These included the Order of the Elephant, strictly the property of Denmark, and long and involved negotiations followed before the insignia could be returned to Copenhagen.

These conditions do not apply to the lower classes of orders, in which cases the insignia remains the property of the recipients or their heirs. The demand for such items varies according to the class or division of the order. The Order of the British Empire, which is the one most commonly found, illustrates this clearly. The breast star of the K.B.E. worn by a Knight of the Order rates more highly than the collar decoration of a C.B.E. (Commander), which in turn is more in demand than the crosses worn by Officers or Members of the Order.

Awards in the Military Division are more highly regarded than those in the Civil Division, though much depends on the person who received the award. The M.B.E. awarded to a political worker for long and faithful service on his district party committee would not appeal to a collector in the way that a military M.B.E. would, particularly if it formed part of an interesting group. On the other hand, were an M.B.E. awarded to one of the Beatles to come on the market, it is presumed that the 'lay interest' involved would raise its value considerably. It is curious to recall how, at the time of the controversial award of this decoration to the pop-singers, a number of earnest individuals who had won the order in less glamorous circumstances made a show of returning their decorations to the Central Chancery as a protest against the debasement of the award.

FOREIGN MEDALS AND DECORATIONS

The interest in, and consequent demand for, foreign medals and decorations is a lot less in Britain for several reasons, the main one being that in most cases these awards are not named to the recipient. Thus it is extremely difficult to assign medals and decorations to the proper recipient and virtually impossible to build up the sort of background story which endears his medals to the collector. The absence of records comparable to British medal and muster rolls, or the relative inaccessibility of them, are further obstacles in the way of the serious collector. It is significant that foreign awards are seldom offered in groups by dealers and, in general, where they are collected, it is sufficient to form a type collection. This is a rather barren exercise for which the exotic appearance of many of these awards is a poor compensation.

Another factor militating against the popularity of foreign awards is the greater liberality with which many of them have been doled out. The French Légion d'Honneur and the Croix de Guerre, the American Bronze Star and Purple Heart, and the German Iron Cross are notorious examples and even the respective highest awards (the Médaille Militaire, the Congressional Medal of Honor and the Ordre Pour la Mérite) have always been more plentiful than the Victoria Cross. Incidentally, a great many Medals of Honor were awarded in the Korean War (1950–4) and already 21 have been won in Vietnam in the two years since the war there has involved American troops on a large scale.

One notable exception to the general apathy for foreign medals is the somewhat perverse interest shown in Nazi decorations. In this case, however, the demand comes not so much from medal collectors as such, but from those who find some vicarious thrill in the trappings of the Hitler régime. Even so, there seem to be plenty of Iron Crosses and Eastern Front campaign medals around to satisfy everyone who wants them and though the price of Nazi medals has hardened in recent years (as it has for all types of material) it is still possible to pick them up for less than a pound apiece. Even the impressive Knight's Cross with crossed swords and oak-leaves can be found for under £15.

CONDITION

The same terms are applied to describe the condition of

medals as apply to coins, though the wear to which the former are subject is usually caused by other factors. In modern times, when the number of occasions on which medals are worn are few and far between, the condition of most items will be found to be VF to EF; indeed, in many cases, the medals may never have been worn at all. A good proportion of Second World War medals and decorations are found in almost mint condition since they were not issued till long after the war, by which time their recipients had been demobilised. In some cases they even turn up still in the original cardboard box in which they were posted to the recipients.

Before the First World War, however, the wearing of medals was customary on all but the most informal occasions and when actually serving on active duty. Thus medals could be, and often were, subject to a great deal of wear. It will be found that the reverse side of these medals is usually considerably more worn than the obverse (or upper) side, on account of the constant rubbing against the tunic. Medals worn by cavalry-men are often found in poor condition, with scratches and edge knocks occasioned by the constant jangling on horseback. Often the medals in a group have an abrasive effect on each other. For this reason the Queen's Medal for Egypt (1881) is comparatively rare in excellent condition, since it was usually worn in juxtaposition to the Khedive's Star whose points were capable of doing considerable damage. Apart from these factors it should also be remembered that part of the ritual of 'spit and polish' involved one's medals and they were often submitted to vigorous cleaning with metal polish.

For these reasons medals are often sold by dealers 'as worn'— a euphemism which conceals a lifetime of hardy service on the chest of some grizzled veteran. But, because of the strong personal element involved in medal-collecting, genuine wear does not affect the value of a medal to the same degree that it would in other branches of numismatics. There is even a school of thought which considers that such signs enhance the interest and value of a medal. This line of thinking also explains the controversy over medal ribbons.

Military outfitters still carry extensive stocks of ribbons

covering every campaign from Waterloo onwards so that it is a very easy matter to obtain a fresh length of ribbon for any medal requiring it, and there is no doubt that the appearance of a piece is greatly enhanced by a nice, clean, bright new ribbon. On the other hand, that ribbon was not the one actually worn by Corporal Bloggs on parade and, to the purist, it would spoil the total effect of the medal. Some collectors therefore treasure the original ribbon, even though it may be faded and frayed. As ribbons are things which one cannot authenticate, however, there seems to me to be little material benefit to be gained from clinging rigidly to a tattered strip of silk when an identical piece can be obtained for a few pence.

Medals have sometimes been put to uses other than those for which they were produced and consequently bear the marks of their conversion. They may be found with pin and clasp mounts converting them into brooches. They may be found with silver 'feet' and brackets transforming them into menu stands (a favourite device at one time). In neither case will the self-respecting collector show any interest in them, though I regret to say that I have occasionally seen such bastard pieces offered for sale by dealers. These items have been spoiled beyond redemption and are worth no more than their scrap value.

Sources of Information

Reference books on medals and decorations are relatively few but those which are available will be found very helpful. First in the field is J. H. Mayo's *Medals and Decorations of the British Army and Navy*, published in two volumes in 1897. This is quite comprehensive and useful, but superseded to a large extent by *British Battles and Medals* by Major L. L. Gordon, which has run to three editions between 1947 and 1962 and is the 'bible' of medal collectors. It gives an encyclopaedic mass of information, often listing the names of all known recipients of the scarcer bars (under 25 as a rule). Books dealing with a specific decoration and tracing the biographies of its recipients include *The Story of the Victoria Cross* by Brigadier Sir John Smyth (himself a holder of the V.C.), and *The George Cross*, by Lieut.-Colonel Ian Bisset.

Captain Tapprell-Dorling's book *Ribbons and Medals* first appeared as a slim paper-back during the First World War, but has been reprinted and greatly expanded on many occasions and now provides a succinct guide to the medals and decorations of the world, with some emphasis on British awards. Books in the English language dealing with foreign medals include L. L. Babin's *Japanese War Medals, Orders and Decorations* and J. A. Sawicki's *Nazi Decorations and Medals*, 1933–45. Paul Hieronymussen's *Orders, Medals and Decorations of Britain and Europe* deals with gallantry awards, decorations and orders of chivalry, but not with campaign medals. Several European countries are covered by works devoted to them individually. Of these the best is probably *Décorations Officielles Françaises*, published by the French government in 1956. Belgium and the Netherlands are covered by *Recueil Illustre des Ordres de Chevalrie et Decorations Belges de 1830 à 1963*, by H. Quinot and *De Nederlandse Ridderorden en Onderscheidingen* by Dr. W. F. Bax. Other useful reference books are A. Berghman's *Nordiska Riddereordnar och Dekorationer* (Norway) and A. W. Hazelton's *Russian Imperial Orders*. The United States is catered for in B. L. Belder's *United States War Medals*, while the decorations of a country which now forms the fiftieth state of the Union are dealt with in G. Medcalf's *Hawaian Royal Orders, Insignia, Classes, Regulations and Members*. Stanley Johnson's *The Medal Collector*, published in 1920 is rather dated, but casts an interesting light on collecting habits and the prices obtained fifty years ago.

Where to Find Medals

When I was a schoolboy in Glasgow (not so many years ago) and first began to take an interest in war medals and decorations, I used to visit Barrowland, the famous street market in the east end of the city, and there one could pick up an astonishing range of items, lying unconsidered among piles of otherwise undistinguished junk. At that time it was possible to buy medals with quite rare or unusual bar combinations for their scrap value; there was apparently no numismatic market to speak of and I was thus able to buy some very attractive pieces for ridiculous sums—never more than 10s. on any one purchase.

Pawn shops in that district of Glasgow were then almost as common as public-houses (there may well have been some connection) and their window-displays of unredeemed pledges were another fruitful source of fine material. A very common item, which could be picked up for no more than a shilling or two, was the Irish bronze medal awarded somewhat late in the day (1942) to members of the I.R.A. who fought the British between 1917 and 1921. This rather crudely executed medal, with its heavily armed gunman on the obverse and its black and tan ribbon, no doubt found its way in large quantities to Glasgow in the pockets of labourers who seem to have been only too ready to relieve themselves of it for the sake of a dram.

By contrast, only the other day, while I was standing at the counter of one of London's best known coin dealer's shops an elderly gentleman walked in and asked what the dealer would give him for his medal. Whereupon he produced a small green box containing the I.R.A. medal, in mint, unworn condition, together with its citation. I did not hear the end of the story, since the shop assistant had apparently never heard of this medal, let alone seen it before, so the Irishman was asked to come back later when the proprietor himself would be available. I have no doubt, however, that the possessor of the medal got a fair price for it, while the dealer probably found a ready customer at two or three pounds. The interesting point about this anecdote is that an item which is common in one area, for special economic or geographic reasons, may be scarce or unheard of elsewhere and the regional difference can thus be reflected in the market value of the medal.

In these days of the Welfare State and the affluent society, pawn-shops are not as common as they once were, nor does one readily find medals in any quantity in those that are left. Countless medals must have been consigned to the melting pot in the past and, with the increased popularity of this branch of numismatics, the number of items available for the new collector is getting steadily smaller. Even junk-shops seem to be fewer than at one time, while the more select 'antique shops'

PLATE VIII

<small>An Interesting Medal Group</small>

Distinguished Service Order (1916), Sudan Medal (1898), Africa G.S. Medal with bars for Jubaland, East Africa 1905, Nandi 1905–06 and Somaliland 1908–10, 1914–15 Star, War Medal, Victory Medal with oak leaves (Mentioned in Despatches), Khedive's Sudan Medal and Order of the Star of Zanzibar.

tend to put an inflated value on such medals as they have for sale.

One fruitful source still remains—the house auction. Sales of the contents of country houses are not as numerous as they once were, but nevertheless they often yield interesting material. For the same reason auctioneers in the provinces, who occasionally hold special numismatic sales, sometimes come up with lots of value to the medal collector. A recent example of this was a sale held in February 1968 by Henry Spencer & Sons of Retford, Nottinghamshire, which contained a group of six medals including a D.S.O. (£31) and a General Service Medal with the rare bar 'Bombard Southern Desert Iraq' of 1918 which fetched the remarkable sum of £60. Medals are, of course, featured regularly in the auctions conducted by Glendining's, Christie's and Sotheby's.

Relatively few numismatic dealers cater to the medal collector to any extent, the chief ones being Baldwin, Seaby, Spink, Coins and Medals, and D. J. Crowther in London and the Collectors' Shop (W. Ferris) and A. D. Hamilton, both of Glasgow. At the moment, there is only one dealer who specialises exclusively in medals and decorations and that is John Hayward of Empire House, Piccadilly, London. Hayward has handled at least three Victoria Crosses during the past year and holds the largest and most comprehensive stock of medals in the United Kingdom.

CHAPTER VIII

TOKENS AND JETONS

SINCE 1947, when Britain abandoned the use of silver in the higher denominations of her coins, the majority of pieces in circulation may properly be regarded as no more than token currency. In its strictest sense a token is merely a promise or a symbol of something else which *has* real value. The value inherent in a token is not the thing itself but what it stands for. So long as it is issued and received in good faith and its users trust the promise implied by it, it is of little importance what metal or material it is made of. In a sense, *all* coinage is token in nature since it represents wealth in the form of land or cattle or property. As primitive societies became more sophisticated, barter of goods gave way to the use of coins, though these were vested with a recognisable value on account of their metallic content. Now we have become even more sophisticated and apparently do not require the assurance which precious metals gave to currency of early times. Thus few of the coins in circulation today have any intrinsic value, in any way connected with their face value and it is odd to think that, because of the scrap value of their respective metallic content, a bronze penny is worth more than a cupro-nickel shilling!

In the numismatic sense, however, the term 'token' is used to denote a piece of money of limited validity, an *ersatz* piece brought into being as a result of a shortage of real currency. Throughout history there have been many instances where a dearth of government coinage has led to the issue of substitute coinage by local tradesmen or municipal authorities. In many cases government issues have been confined to the higher denominations, struck in silver or gold, and it has been left to the local authorities to strike small denomination coins in base metal. Thus, during the Roman Imperial period many towns and cities of the Empire continued to mint copper coins for local use. These items are usually treated by numismatists as coins, though strictly speaking they are only tokens or 'money of necessity', so it is difficult to know where to draw the line between the two. Token coinage makes up in historical, political or social interest what it may lack aesthetically, while the fact that most pieces were produced in substances other than precious metals is irrelevant in the assessment of their value. There are several categories of tokens, both those used in place of coins and those which served other purposes.

OBSIDIONAL CURRENCY

One of the less obvious privations suffered by the besieged defenders of a town or city was a shortage of cash, particularly of the smaller denominations. In such uncertain times there would be a tendency for people who possessed good money to hoard it and perhaps even conceal it carefully as a precaution in case the city were overrun by its attackers. Thus good money would rapidly vanish from circulation and such limited commercial activity as was still possible under the strain of siege would be seriously hampered by the lack of currency with which to carry out minor transactions. In times like these the civic authorities would resort to the emergency issues of tokens, known to numismatists as obsidional (from Latin *obsidium*=a siege) currency.

Perhaps the best known examples in Britain are the siege pieces produced during the Civil War. When the Roundheads besieged Newark in 1645–6, the defenders melted down silver plate and fashioned crude coins in denominations of ninepence, shilling and halfcrown. The town of Scarborough produced tokens at this period in the rather odd values of sevenpence and 3s. 4d. Among the pieces produced by the Royalists in Pontefract was a coin issued after the execution of King Charles I and bearing the title of Charles II—probably the first piece to acknowledge the young king. Carlisle and Colchester also produced siege money, the latter being extremely rare nowadays. The Royalists in Ireland also produced several interesting examples of siege money. Many-sided coins were stamped from silver plate by Murrough O'Brien, Lord Inchiquin in 1643. These were in denominations of threepence, fourpence (groat), sixpence, ninepence, shilling and halfcrown, though, in fact, they were stamped with their *weight*, rather than the denomination and thus, strictly speaking, should not be regarded as tokens. Incidentally, Lord Inchiquin also produced gold pieces stamped 4dwt.7gr. on both sides, which passed in currency as equivalent to the French pistole. This is in fact the only example of a gold coin produced in Ireland.

Most obsidional currency, however, consisted of tokens in the true sense, with the implied promise that they would be redeemed in real money when the siege was lifted. During the siege of Leyden in 1574 the Dutch burghers produced leather tokens cut out of the bindings of books. Tokens made from wood or porcelain were produced in Germany towards the end of the First World War and even for two or three years afterwards when wartime conditions were still prevailing. Bronze sous were struck in the besieged cities of Antwerp (1814) and Strasbourg (1814–15) under the authority of Napoleon. Such items are now greatly sought after.

Token coinage of this nature, produced in the stress of war, possesses a great deal of charm on account of the primitive circumstances in which it was produced and the hardships which necessitated it. Like war medals, siege tokens have an element of 'human interest' which sets them apart from other numismatic fields. Consequently these pieces tend to fetch a high price on the infrequent occasions when they turn up in the saleroom.

SPURIOUS PIECES

Tokens have been in use in Britain on many occasions in the past six hundred years, though for different reasons. The earliest of these were the *lushburgs* of the fourteenth century, basemetal counterfeits thought to have emanated from Luxembourg, which flooded the country and rapidly got into circulation among the population which was too illiterate or simple-minded to appreciate the difference between them and good, honest *easterling* (or sterling) coins. Piers Plowman described these 'lusshe-borwes' looking 'lyke asterlynge'. Though the government of the time reacted promptly and savagely against those who imported base coinage and circulated it, the practice continued unabated for more than a century. Examples of 'black money' (as these pieces were called on account of the tarnish on them) are comparatively rare nowadays. The *dodkins*, or *doitkins*, the *pollards*, *crocards*, *suskins*, *turneys* and *galley halfpence* of the late Middle Ages vanished for the most part into the melting pot when they were impounded and condemned by the magistrate and *genuine* examples of these spurious items are now seldom met with. These spurious pieces should not, however, be confused with counterfeits of actual coins. Counterfeits or forgeries are in a different category altogether and as they have been produced either to deceive the populace or (more likely in modern times) the collector, their numismatic interest and value is much more problematical. Since the appearance of the unique 1952 halfcrown several attempts to fake the date on halfcrowns have been reported.

TRADERS' TOKENS

The best known tokens of all are those which were produced in large quantities at various times between the middle of the seventeenth century and the early years of the nineteenth. They fall into three distinct periods each of which has been well-documented and has a keen following among numismatists.

Token farthings and halfpence in copper supplied a need which the regal coinage neglected until the recoinage of 1672, in which copper coins of lower denominations than the penny were introduced. During the brief period (about 26 years) when they were in use, tokens were struck by shop-keepers and merchants, by authorities both municipal and ecclesiastical, and by the proprietors of inns and hostelries. It has been estimated that between 15,000 and 20,000 different types of token were issued and fresh varieties are continually turning up. Technically many of these pieces were quite crude, sometimes inscribed with no more than the date and the initials of the issuer. Others are more elaborate, particularly those struck by towns and cities, and often depict the civic coat of arms or some prominent local building. The inn-keepers' tokens are extremely interesting with their inn-signs on one side and the denomination or other relevant details on the other side. Countless tradesmen produced their own halfpence and farthings which were used in change for their customers. Often these items were 'payable through the neighbourhood, though seldom reaching farther than the next street or two', as the diarist, John Evelyn, described them. Parochial they may have been, but for this very reason they are in great demand, not so much by numismatists, but by local historians and antiquaries. They shed an interesting light on life in the seventeenth-century England of the Commonwealth and the period immediately following the Restoration.

A comprehensive collection of seventeenth-century tokens relating to London, Westminster and Southwark is to be found in the Guildhall Museum. The nucleus of this remarkable collection consisted of more than 1,300 tokens accumulated by H. B. Hanbury Beaufoy and presented to the City over a century ago. Since then it has been greatly added to and is now the largest collection of its kind outside the British Museum. Being confined solely to London and its environs, however, it is in many respects finer and more detailed than the national collection. Every known example of the large brass pennies struck by traders and coffee house proprietors is included, while the exceptionally rare tokens struck on leather are well represented. A catalogue of the collection was compiled by J. H. Burn and published in 1853. This led the way for the definitive work on traders' tokens by Boyne which, in turn, was superseded by the great two-volume *Trade Tokens Issued in the Seventeenth Century* produced by G. C. Williamson in 1899. Reasonable examples of seventeenth century tokens could be picked up not so long ago for a few shillings, but now they fetch as many pounds, such is the tremendous demand for them.

Private enterprise was curbed by the Royal Proclamation of August 1672 when it was ordained that 'all persons, who should after the first day of September make, vend or utter any other kind of pence, halfpence or farthing, or other piece of brass, copper or other base metal, other than the coins authorised above, or should offer to counterfeit any of His Majesty's halfpence or farthings, were to be chastised with exemplary severity.' Nevertheless it appears that trade tokens were tolerated a few years longer, but by 1680 they had become a thing of the past. Little more than a century later, however, history repeated itself. The issue of government coppers was conducted on a half-hearted basis throughout the reigns of the first two Georges (1714–60). None at all was struck between 1755 and 1769, a few were minted in 1770–5 and no coppers from then until 1797 when the 'cartwheels' made their debut.

The shortage of small change was met by the Parys Mine Company of Anglesey which began minting halfpennies and pennies in 1787. This copper mine had been worked sporadically since Roman times and the tokens alluded to a famous landmark in the history of the island, by depicting on the obverse the portrait of a Druid. It was here that the Druids, the pagan priests of ancient Britain, made their last stand in the first century A.D. The Anglesey coppers were an instant success and their use was widespread in Wales and North-West England. Soon they were being emulated by tokens struck in other parts of the country and by the end of the century they numbered many thousands of different varieties. Unlike their seventeenth century predecessors, they were usually well produced and rather larger in size, thus offering more scope to the artist who designed them. Many of them were beautiful examples of medallic art, quite consciously pictorial and towards the end of the period when they were current there is no doubt that some of them were produced for the numismatic cabinet rather than for genuine usage.

These elegant pieces, with their representations of the great new buildings, which were a visible sign of the greater affluence of the country with the advent of the Industrial Revolution, vied with the more humdrum types which served as advertisements for manufacturers of a wide range of new consumer goods. The multiplicity of different subjects depicted on these tokens has led collectors to specialise along geographical or thematic lines. Tokens showing places in London appeared in great profusion, but other cities, notably Bath and Bristol, produced many fine tokens, while county collections have been a popular pastime.

Tokens associated with specific subjects or professions are avidly collected not only by numismatists but by students of other fields. Postal historians have long been interested in the handsome Bath tokens honouring its illustrious citizen, John Palmer, the postal reformer who introduced the mail coach in 1784. Mail coach halfpennies were also issued by some of the more important hostelries, such as the famous *Swan with Two Necks* in Lad Lane, London. Other tokens feature celebrities and local worthies, figures in folklore and national heroes. The token, like the commemorative medal, was even used as a medium for political propaganda and patriotic sentiment (particularly during the French Revolutionary Wars). An interesting example of a political token is illustrated by C. C. Chamberlain in his *Guide to Numismatics*. It depicts a map of France on the obverse being trampled under the naked foot of a revolutionary, with the word RELIGION broken up and the word GLORY partially erased. The other side bears a stirring slogan containing a numismatic pun—MAY GREAT BRITAIN EVER REMAIN THE REVERSE.

Towards the end of the century, however, the unduly prolific output of new tokens began to affect their popularity and it is a matter for conjecture that, had the regal coppers not appeared in 1797 and done away with the need for tokens, they would have died out eventually. More and more tokens were produced in deliberately limited editions which savour of some of the questionable practices of the recent gold medal craze. Consequently many of these collector's pieces turn up in mint condition and, while most attractive to look at, undeniably lack the charm of the earlier pieces which fulfilled the function for which they were originally intended.

There was a genuine, but brief, resurgence of tokens in the nineteenth century. The industrial expansion which took place during the Napoleonic Wars and the creation of a great urban proletariat earning larger wages than ever before, put a tremendous strain on the resources of the Mint. Prior to the Great Recoinage of 1816–17, when our existing coins first appeared, several expedients were resorted to in order to alleviate the shortage. A vast quantity of Spanish dollars was countermarked by the Bank of England in 1804 and put into circulation as five-shilling tokens. Seven years later silver tokens were issued by the Bank in denominations of three shillings or eighteen pence and numerous big industrial concerns also released silver tokens consisting of Spanish dollars usually countermarked with the denomination and the name of the factory or mill concerned.

Smaller denominations, ranging from sixpence to three shillings, were struck in silver by private firms. Banks in Ireland, the Channel Islands, the Isle of Man and several of the larger cities produced some interesting and handsome tokens. Many of them bore the effigy of the king on the obverse and were not unlike the regal coins in other respects. Because these tokens were comparatively numerous they are not as expensive to buy nowadays as the countermarked factory dollars. Most of the nineteenth century silver tokens appeared between 1804 and 1817 when they were declared illegal and replaced by the regal shillings, halfcrowns and sixpences in the size and weight which have been retained to the present day.

Copper or bronze penny tokens were also produced in this brief period. These are of a rather more serious, utilitarian nature than the elegant *fin de siècle* pieces, and are often to be found with an inscription on the reverse, to the effect that the tradesman issuing them will redeem 240 of them for 'a pound note.'

Traders' tokens did not disappear entirely from the social and commercial scene. Meal tokens (the ancestors of today's luncheon vouchers) were issued in the mid-nineteenth century, not by benevolent employers but by the coldly charitable Inspectors of the Poor and the Work-houses; and tokens which could be exchanged for goods from the factory shop were issued to workers until the Truck Acts of the 1830s stamped out this subtle form of exploitation. Before the era of trading stamps it was not an uncommon practice for grocers to give tokens, or 'checks' to their customers as a form of discount. These pieces were often made of plastic or thin metal discs and had no pretensions to art whatsoever. So far as I am aware no one has yet taken the trouble to make a collection of these modern, utilitarian tokens, but they may eventually be of interest to the social historian of the future. It is interesting to have in mind that one of the chief issuers of modern times has been the co-operative stores.

Token coinage was not unique to Britain, although the greatest variety of tokens was issued there. Another, though not so prolific, issuer of tokens was Canada which suffered an acute shortage of low value coinage in the early nineteenth century. Copper tokens were imported in vast quantities from England at the end of the Napoleonic period. Among the most popular were the Tiffin Tokens, named after Joseph Tiffin, a Montreal merchant who first put them into circulation in 1812–13. They portrayed King George III on the obverse and bore an allegorical figure of Commerce on the reverse. A puzzling item from this period is a token inscribed SHIPS COLONIES & COMMERCE; this token circulated in lieu of a halfpenny in Prince Edward Island and alluded to the three factors which Napoleon predicted would give Britain the ultimate advantage over him. Many of these tokens were counterfeited in brass, but were themselves apparently accepted as currency, so great was the shortage of regal coinage.

By 1835 the Canadian banks had begun to take the initiative and were issuing their own token sous and halfpence. The issues of the Bank of Montreal, la Banque du Peuple, the Banks of Upper and Lower Canada and the Quebec Bank were often handsome and technically competent, being for the most part minted by the Midland firms of Boulton and Watt, and Heaton & Co. Designs by Pistrucci and the Wyons were used for some of these attractive tokens. Many of them can still be picked up for less than a pound, although they tend to be more expensive on the other side of the Atlantic, where Whitman's standard catalogue of Canadian coinage gives them great prominence.

Few countries have not produced tokens at some time or another. The First World War and the immediate postwar years witnessed the proliferation of tokens in Europe, particularly in France where they ranged from the government tokens for 1 and 2 francs and 50 centimes to the humbler pieces issued by tradesmen. The government issues, produced by the French Chamber of Commerce and replacing the regular silver coins of the Sower type, featured the allegorical figure of Commerce and incorporated the inscription 'BON POUR' (Good for) followed by the denomination. These brass tokens are still exceedingly plentiful and quite passable specimens will be found in every dealer's mixture trays. Much harder to find, however, are the other classes of token and even relatively common examples in F condition rate a few shillings upwards.

Germany also produced a few tokens but this unfortunate country was swiftly overtaken by hyper-inflation which reduced the value of the mark to microscopic proportions. By mid-1923 the astronomical sum of 50,000,000,000 marks would have purchased little more than a box of matches. The value of the mark plummeted so fast that workmen were paid twice a day. It was impossible to keep pace with the mark by issuing tokens, let alone a government coinage and paper money was resorted to. The fascinating story of *notgeld*, as this emergency money was called, is told in the next chapter.

TRANSPORT TOKENS

A fairly restricted class of token consists of those which were produced for use on trains, buses and trams. In a sense, therefore, their purpose was two-fold: they represented a certain sum of money and served in place of the more familiar paper or card tickets of the present day. These tokens could be bought at a booking office and surrendered to the collector on boarding the conveyance or at the end of the journey. In this respect they differed in no way from the modern tickets. The fact that they were produced in metal, often circular in shape and struck like coins, has long commended them to numismatists. Furthermore there is evidence that, since they represented a certain amount of money, they were actually circulated to some extent as a form of token coinage. This is particularly true of Canada, France and the Low Countries. Many of the French and Belgian specimens from the First World War era bear the signs of frequent circulation which indicate their use as money of necessity. Examples in fine condition are usually hard to find and, because of their connection with communications, are much in demand by railway enthusiasts and transport historians. Some of these tokens not only bore the name of the railway or bus company but bore a representation of a locomotive or tram-car, which greatly enhances their value. Most of them were struck in bronze, brass, aluminium or some other base metal, but railway passes, intended for the use of directors of the railway companies and other privileged individuals, were usually struck in silver.

Such tokens, conveying the right of free travel over the company's lines for a certain period, are highly sought after and correspondingly expensive. A few were even named personally or even struck specially on behalf of some particularly privileged person and these items rank among the great rarities of the token world.

At the other extreme are the tokens, sometimes in base metal but more recently manufactured in different colours of plastic, given to municipal employees, postmen, etc. for use on corporation buses or trams. These tokens usually bear the figure of value on the reverse and sometimes show the civic arms on the obverse. Their use is not so general as it once was, so they may have some antiquarian value some day. At the moment they are generally disregarded by numismatists, though not, however, overlooked by the transport historian.

A further example of tokens are the *jetons* still used in Paris telephones.

STAMPS USED AS TOKENS

Postage stamps were declared legal tender in the United Kingdom during both World Wars, but so far as I am aware they were never actually used as a form of token coinage in this country. There was never a shortage of small change such as beset other countries at various times. In these circumstances, however, stamps were resorted to as a form of currency and examples of this sort are highly sought after by philatelists, though overlooked to some extent by numismatists.

During the American Civil War the banks suspended specie payments with the result that such coins as were in circulation were jealously hoarded and soon vanished from the commercial scene. This situation was impossible. Shopkeepers were unable to give small change to their customers and inevitably a system of barter arose which was highly impracticable. Postage stamps constituted a form of currency ready to hand and, for a time, they circulated as a substitute for nickels and dimes. In New York City alone the sale of stamps rose from $3,000 daily to $16,000. Unfortunately stamps are fragile things which do not tolerate too much handling. Before long they were dog-eared and unrecognisable, and therefore valueless as 'coins'.

It was then that J. Gault, a Boston sewing-machine salesman, came up with the brilliant idea of encasing stamps in small circular metal discs, rather like coins, but with a mica front through which the face of the stamp would be visible. Gault's idea spread like wildfire; at last the public had something which looked and felt like a coin, and a handful of them even had something of the jingle of the coins which were so sadly missed.

The encased stamps, furthermore, had the added advantage over the former coins in that they provided space for enterprising merchants—and the American ad-man of a century ago was just as enterprising as his presentday counterpart, judging from the numerous varieties of advertisements found stamped or engraved on the backs of these discs. The stamps used were the definitive series of 1861 and denominations ranging from 1 to 90 cents were used. An unusual 'multiple token' was the rectangle enclosing a strip of three 3 cents stamps to make a 9 cent 'coin'. Friedberg's *Paper Money of the United States* records almost 200 varieties of encased postage stamps, with many combinations of advertisement ranging from patent medicines to life assurance.

The value of these encased tokens depends not only on the stamp itself but on the advertisement on the back. Surprisingly,

only Gault himself is known to have used 2 cents stamps
('Black Jacks') and these are the rarest of all the encased items,
being valued at over $300. Even the cheapest variety—the
1 cent piece advertising Ayer's Cathartic Pills—catalogues at
$4.50, since there is a great demand in the United States for
such tokens, by numismatists and philatelists alike. The use of
encased stamps was short-lived, however, and they were soon
eclipsed by the government issues of Postage Currency. As these
notes depicting representations of postage stamps were really
paper money they are more appropriate to the next chapter.

Encased stamps were used as currency at the end of the First
World War. Prior to the inflation period of 1922–3 in Germany
and Austria the shortage of coins was met by encasing postage
stamps in a similar fashion to the American tokens of sixty years
earlier. These mica-faced discs are larger than the American
type, about the size of a penny, and were backed by either
aluminium or plastic. Likewise they carried a wide range of
advertisements. The practice spread to France, also experien-
cing an acute shortage of specie. The French discs sometimes
have a numeral on the reverse indicating their value. The use of
these makeshifts even extended to former neutrals, such as
Norway, Denmark and Argentina, while Belgium, Greece and
Italy also used them to some extent. Examples from countries
other than Austria, Germany and France are extremely scarce
and even the common varieties from the former are now worth
over a pound apiece.

Stamps have also been circulated in lieu of coins, by sticking
them to special cards. The British South Africa Company in
Rhodesia adopted this measure to alleviate the shortage of
coins in 1900 during the Boer War. Small cards measuring 5.5
by 7.5 cms. were issued during this period by the Civil Commissioners at Bulawayo. They bore the statement: 'Please pay in
cash to the person producing this card the face value of the
stamp affixed thereto, if presented on or after the 1st August,
1900. This card must be produced for redemption not later than
1st October, 1900. (Signed) H. Marshal Hole, Secretary.'

These cards bear the imprint of the Chronicle Printing Works,
Bulawayo and a great variety of rubber stamps were used to

authenticate the Secretary's signature. On the back, stamps of the British South Africa Company were affixed. Those recorded so far are the 3d., 6d., 1s., 2s., 2s. 6d. and 10s. stamps of the period. Of the £20,000 worth issued, about £1,000 were never redeemed and it must be presumed that the quantity of stamped cards in the hands of collectors must be fairly small.

An extension of this idea was the re-issue in 1915 of three of the Romanov commemorative stamps by Russia, printed on stout card and inscribed 'On par with silver currency' on the back. These were the 10, 15 and 20 kopeck denominations and they could, of course, be used either as money or for the payment of postage, but in genuine postally used condition—especially on the original envelopes—they are quite elusive. In 1917 the Kerensky government treated the 1, 2 and 3 kopeck stamps in similar fashion, some of the 1 and 2 kopeck values being surcharged '1' or '2' across the face of the stamp in addition. Stamps printed on card for use as currency appeared at the end of the First World War in some of the fragments of the erstwhile Russian Empire. The ephemeral régimes of the Don Cossacks, Armenia, the Crimea and the Ukraine produced various stamps in 1918–20 printed on ungummed paper or thick card with inscriptions on the reverse authorising their use as coins. As an alternative to encased postage stamps Austria also produced cardboard stamps in 1919–20 for use as money tokens. The use of this device was much more limited during the Second World War, examples being confined to the Indian state of Bundi where 3 pies and 1 anna tokens made of card depicted the current stamps overprinted 'Cash coupon—Bundi State.' Filipino guerillas operating in Japanese occupied territory in 1942 produced 5 peso notes to which revenue stamps of the appropriate amount were affixed.

Stamps mounted on card in the Rhodesian manner were used in Madagascar during the First World War and were issued officially by the Bureau des Postes, in denominations from 5c. to 2 frs. Turkey used postage, fiscal and railway stamps backed by yellowish paper for a time at the end of the First World War in lieu of metal coinage. During the Spanish Civil War a shortage of small coins was met by the Republican Government who consequently issued stamps of the definitive series affixed to cardboard discs bearing the Spanish coat of arms on the reverse.

With the exception of the Russian card-stamps none of these cases listed are common and even the Russian examples which, till quite recently, could be bought for coppers are rapidly disappearing. The stamps of Rhodesia, Madagascar and Spain mounted on card are seldom found in mint condition and even those which bear the signs of frequent circulation will cost upwards of a pound each when they turn up. Really fine specimens can be worth £5 or more, depending to some extent on the particular stamp shown on them. Even now, however, these items are underpriced, bearing in mind their comparative rarity. They fall between the two stools of numismatics and philately and are largely disregarded by students of both subjects as being not quite stamps and not quite coins. Nevertheless they have a legitimate interest to both hobbies and with increasing publicity they are likely to rise in value quite sharply. Ignorance of these items in both the numismatic and philatelic trade accounts for the lack of interest to some extent, though this permits the knowledgeable collector to pick up unconsidered bargains.

Because they are listed and priced in both numismatic and stamp catalogues (the Friedberg and Scott hand-books respectively) the American encased stamps have an established value and are keenly sought after by numismatists and philatelists accordingly. There is no corresponding catalogue for the French or German encased stamps and their existence—and rarity—is little appreciated outside their own countries. Not so long ago I found a nice example of a French encased stamp—one of the commoner types it is true—in a coin dealer's 6d. tray. When I asked him if he had any more like this he said that he had never seen one before. Yet this particular item has been known to change hands for £2—when it turns up.

JETONS AND COUNTERS

Jetons (from the French word *jeter*, to throw) comprise virtually all the pieces which look like coins and yet were never

PLATE IX

COMMEMORATIVE MEDALS

(1) Coronation, 1911; (2) Admiral Vernon, 1739; (3) English workers' visit to
Paris, 1848; (4) First World War Generals; (5) Glasgow Corporation Coronation
Medal, 1911; (6) Schwyz, 600th anniversary; (7) Glasgow Special Constables',
War Medal, 1918; (8) Ayr School Board Medal, 1886; (9) Secession of the Free
Church of Scotland, 1843.

intended for use as money. The terms jeton and counter are, in fact, synonymous, meaning the small coin-like objects used in medieval accountancy or, in more recent times, as gaming chips.

The earliest jetons appeared in France in the thirteenth century and were employed by clerks in the royal exchequer for computing accounts. Francis Barnard, in *The Casting-Counter and the Counting-Board* records examples from the reign of Philip the Bold (1270–85) and states that many of them were struck in gold or silver as well as in copper. The nobility emulated the king and produced jetons for their own use. The earliest pieces were rather crude in appearance, a cross being a favourite device. Most jetons are round, though a few were rectangular or hexagonal. Jetons coincided with the development of heraldry and they became increasingly ornate, depicting coats of arms and other symbols (a pair of scales, emblematic of accountancy, was a favourite device). In the seventeenth and eighteenth centuries great quantities of jetons were manufactured on the Continent for use in gaming and accountancy and they resemble English trade tokens in many respects (except that they never circulated as coinage). This was a period of elaborate designs; many different subjects, from the artistic to the politically satirical, were featured and some of them were extremely well executed.

Perhaps the best-known example of a British gaming counter is the brass imitation of the Spade Guinea of George III (so-called on account of the shape of the coat of arms on the reverse). The obverse bears the effigy and titles of the king, but on the reverse, surrounding the shield, is the quaint inscription—IN MEMORY OF THE GOOD OLD DAYS. The eighteenth century populace may largely have been illiterate, but at least they knew their brass from their gold. It is a sad commentary on our present economic condition that many people, chancing upon one of these counters, fondly imagine that they have found a Spade Guinea. In an age when gold is not as common as it once was it is easy to understand the confusion.

Another item which causes confusion is the 'Cumberland Jack' which bears more than a passing resemblance to the sovereign. Its exact function is a little obscure; struck in brass, it was often used as a gaming counter, but its resemblance to the sovereign may also have been intended to deceive. Primarily, however, it was a satirical medalet aimed at the unpopular Duke of Cumberland, uncle of Queen Victoria. The Pistrucci St. George on the reverse is replaced by a crowned horseman, representing the Duke, and the inscription TO HANOVER is an allusion to the fact that he succeeded to the throne of that country in place of his niece who was debarred from inheriting it, under Salic Law, on account of her sex. The original 'Jacks' were dated 1837, the year in which the reactionary Prince George took possession of his new kingdom, but other dates are found (usually 1830 or 1833) on later issues which were fraudulently passed off as sovereigns. The fraud should have been immediately apparent since the obverse portrayed Queen Victoria who was only eleven years old in 1830. These pieces are still very common and possess little interest or value to numismatists.

Other items about which little is known are miniature replicas of coins, sometimes inscribed MODEL COIN. They were produced as counters for various games and also as novelties, in Victorian Christmas crackers. The so-called Model Penny, a small bronze piece with a tiny silver plug in the centre, was actually produced by a Birmingham manufacturer, Joseph Moore, as a suggestion for improving the coinage. This is a minor branch of numismatics which few collectors regard seriously; yet it is an interesting field which would repay the serious student since the material is not very hard to find.

Until 1963 the silver dollar was popular in American gambling casinos as a gaming counter, but with the rapid disappearance of these large silver coins the proprietors of these establishments have been forced to produce counters of their own. The sudden dearth of the 'cartwheel' posed a serious problem to the owners of the dollar slot-machines. They tried defacing the remaining coins to render them useless to collectors, but instead they fell foul of the U.S. Treasury whose regulations forbade such practices. Likewise the import of Canadian silver dollars for use in gaming machines was promptly squashed by Federal and State authorities. An attempt by the Nevada club proprietors to force Washington to mint more dollars in 1964 came to nothing.

In desperation the casinos decided to mint their own 'cart-wheel tokens' and negotiations with the Franklin Mint, the main operating division of General Numismatics Corporation of Yeadon, Pennsylvania, were concluded in July 1964 when Harrah's Casino at Lake Tahoe, Nevada, took delivery of the first Franklin tokens. During the following year six other casinos began using these tokens minted in a special, hard-wearing nickel-columbium alloy. Since then a non-magnetic cupro-nickel alloy known as Franklinium 11 has been used, and also an alloy of nickel-brass simulating gold.

For a short period these cartwheel tokens were even accepted by hotels and shops in payment but this has now been curbed by U.S. Treasury regulations and the tokens are strictly used for gaming purposes only. A few clubs have made use of inferior pewter pieces but most casinos in Nevada now use Franklin tokens. By the end of 1965 Franklin tokens were in use in 27 clubs and during 1966 the number increased to 62. Later additions to the range have been cupro-nickel half dollars (necessitated by the fantastic demand by collectors for the Kennedy half-dollar) and a handsome five-dollar token struck in sterling silver. Already the silver $5 pieces have been super-seded by 'clad' tokens, with a sterling silver overlay bonded to a cupro-silver core. The original 'fives' are now greatly prized as collector's pieces.

The use of Franklin tokens has extended to other parts of the American continent and even to Britain, where the Playboy Club in London and the Cavalier Club in Scotland use £1 tokens. The designs of these tokens are many and varied, each casino or club having its own distinctive type, usually depicting the club building or some emblem connected with it. Already these Nevada and associated gaming tokens are catching the interest of numismatists in the United States, although they are as yet little studied or collected in Britain.

LOVE TOKENS

Occasionally one comes across miscellaneous coins in junk

shops which turn out to be not quite what they seemed at first sight. They are coins which have been worn or polished smooth and then engraved with a date and the names of a man or woman (or both). Sometimes a motto or sentimental inscription is added which gives a clue to the purpose of the 'coin'. This practice appears to have been at its height in the eighteenth century, the commonest coins employed being the copper half-pennies of George III (*c.* 1770–5), though Victorian coppers and foreign coins are sometimes found. Base metal coins were most favoured, but occasionally silver or even gold coins were treated in this way.

The names or initials are those of two lovers and the date signifies either the betrothal or the marriage. Pieces have been recorded with inscriptions commemorating an anniversary such as a silver or golden wedding. The addition of cupids, pierced hearts and other symbols of love help the collector to recognise these love tokens at a glance. More rarely one finds elaborate engravings of lovers and courting scenes and the simple motto sometimes gives way to a lengthy inscription running to many words, in which the lover declares his devotion and affection for his mistress.

The style of engraving varies greatly; it ranges from crudely-punched initials in the spaces between the arms of the cruciform shields on the Georgian sixpence to the ornate and finely executed pictures done by an accomplished artist. A popular device, though an extremely tedious one, was 'pin-hole' work in which the engraving was effected by stamping the surface of the coin with a fine-pointed punch; as many as 30 pricks might be required to form a single letter of the inscription. Usually the surface of the coin would be ground to a smooth plane before engraving but often the inscription would merely be added to the blank areas of the field, or engraved round the edge of the coin. Judging by the dates found on them these tokens were at the height of their popularity in the latter half of the eighteenth century, though dated examples as early as 1724 are known, and the practice persisted as late as 1860.

Apart from those tokens exchanged by lovers there are a few cases recorded of other forms of presentation. One elaborate example bears the inscription: 'The gift of my father, W. Joiner, being the only penny he earned on the day of my birth—August 24. 1852.' Births and deaths were recorded in much the same way as marriages.

What was the purpose of these tokens? Surprisingly few of them are found pierced, which seems to indicate that they were not generally intended as ornaments to be worn from a chain or ribbon round the neck (although it should be noted that silver threepences of the Victorian period are found with initials on them and were sometimes made up into bracelets). It would appear from the very worn state in which many of them are found that they were carried in a pocket or purse as a lucky piece.

COMMUNION TOKENS

In the Protestant church, particularly in the Scottish Presbyterian form and occasionally in the French and Dutch Calvinist forms, the sacrament of Communion was preceded by a service of catechism when the members of the flock would be subject to examination on matters moral and spiritual and tested on their knowledge of the Scriptures. This catechising took place on the Thursday preceding the Communion (which was usually held annually) and those who were regarded as fit to attend the Sunday service were given tokens which were subsequently used to gain admittance. They would be handed over to the Kirk elder on duty at the door on the morning of the Communion and thus they may be regarded as a form of ticket.

The earliest Communion tokens, dating in some cases from even before the Reformation of 1560, were of card (as they are nowadays), but by the beginning of the seventeenth century lead tokens were being adopted. These were either cast in a simple mould or stamped out of thin lead sheets. The earliest examples are very crude, rectangular in format and uniface, with often no more than the name (or an abbreviation) of the parish. These primitive pieces were probably the work of the local blacksmith. Many examples, throughout the three centuries when they were in use, were undated and could therefore be used for several years. By the end of the seventeenth century the practice of dating tokens came into fashion. It is sometimes possible to date these early undated tokens reasonably accurately; this is the case where the initials of the Minister are incorporated in the inscription, though this practice itself did not become popular till well into the eighteenth century.

The tokens of the eighteenth and nineteenth centuries became not only more elaborate but better designed and executed. A pictorial element was introduced in the tokens of the wealthier parishes, usually in cities such as Aberdeen, Edinburgh and Glasgow; these may be found embellished with the coat of arms of the city or burgh, or even with a detailed reproduction of the church itself. Religious symbolism is conspicuous by its absence, the Cross and other traditional Christian emblems being taboo in Scottish Presbyterian practice. A rare exception is the cross token of Panbridge (Carnoustie), recorded by the Rev. Thomas Burns in his encyclopaedic treatise, *Old Scottish Communion Plate and Tokens*. The Communion Cup and the Burning Bush, however, are common emblems on the later tokens.

Towards the end of the eighteenth century the custom of adding appropriate verses from the Scriptures became widespread. The commonest inscription is taken from 1 Corinthians, XI, 23: 'This do in remembrance of Me' (the words of Jesus Christ to His Disciples during the Last Supper). Another favourite inscription is 'Let a man examine himself'—referring to the pre-Communion catechism. Sometimes both inscriptions are found on the same token, on the obverse and reverse respectively.

After the Great Secession of 1843, when Thomas Chalmers led his followers out of the Established Church to form the Free Church of Scotland, tokens of the latter sect can be distinguished by their comparative plainness and the inclusion of the date 1843. This tends to confuse the newcomer to the study of Communion tokens since items bearing this date were in use for very many years after that time. In a sense they are commemorative; but genuinely commemorative tokens are comparatively rare. Kettle United Presbyterian Church in Fife produced such a piece in 1878 to mark the centenary of the parish.

Towards the end of the nineteenth century tokens were more usually struck in pewter, though occasionally in bronze or brass and gradually became more uniform in size and design. A lozenge format was most common at this time, though rectangles and circular types are sometimes met with. Diamond and heart-shaped tokens are relatively scarce.

The use of metal tokens gradually died out in the early years of this century, though the custom of distributing tokens survived in at least one parish in the island of Skye till ten years ago and may still be carried on for all I know in some of the remoter parishes of the Highlands and Islands. Surprisingly, the use of metal Communion tokens has continued to flourish in other parts of the world where the Scots emigrants took their form of worship. Some Presbyterian churches in Canada and the United States have produced excellent designs in quite recent years, often of a commemorative nature.

Little interest is excited in Communion tokens outside Scotland and even there they can still be picked up for a few shillings at most. Nevertheless interest seems to be increasing as the prices demonstrate. Not so long ago the majority of items encountered could be purchased for a few pence; now as many shillings are asked and in some cases more than a pound has to be paid, where the token is of outstanding interest or early date. Fine collections of Scottish Communion tokens are housed in the Hunterian and Royal Scottish Museums while the Department of Coins and Medals at the British Museum has a comprehensive collection also.

Literature on the subject is sparse. Apart from the work mentioned above, *The Story of the Token* by Robert Sheills is almost the only handbook available, though detailed articles on aspects of Communion tokens will be found from time to time in the proceedings of the Society of Antiquaries of Scotland.

MISCELLANEOUS TOKENS

Tokens have been produced as tickets of admission to entertainment over a long period. The *spintriae* or *lasciva nomismata*,

referred to by Martial in Book VIII, may have been used as
tickets of admission to Roman brothels. Their designs, which
are highly pornographic, would seem to suggest a usage of this
sort.

Tokens for admission to pleasure gardens such as Ranelagh
or Vauxhall, were used in eighteenth century England. Tokens
were also produced by theatres and given to actors and actresses
as complimentary tickets for use by their friends. Tokens valid
for any performance during the season of a particular play were
manufactured and sold to patrons of the theatre. These were
often struck in silver and bore the name of the theatre and the
play and sometimes had the name of the patron or token-
holder engraved on them. Occasionally the number of the
patron's box or seat was also engraved on them. These tokens
are in great demand by collectors of theatrical material and as
a consequence they tend to be rather expensive, their value
depending on the name of the theatre or the show and also on
the name of the patron if the latter was a famous actor or other
celebrity. Tokens for the entire season were expensive to buy in
the first place and therefore no expense was spared in making
them attractive and substantial. Examples made of ivory are
known, but the usual material was silver. Ordinary theatre
tokens, however, were made of base material, either bronze or
pewter. Tokens of this sort are dealt with in *Tickets and Passes
of Great Britain and Ireland* by W. J. Davis and A. W. Waters.

*   *   *   *   *

A significant indication of the growth of interest in tokens of
all kinds is the greater frequency of articles on various aspects
of this branch of numismatics in the general periodicals. There
is no specialised journal in Britain, however, devoted to tokens.
The gap is filled to a large extent by the excellent journal of the
Token and Medal Society, available from Russell Rulau,
Sidney, Ohio. This American society has a world-wide membership and caters to collectors interested in all forms of tokens and
commemorative medals.

CHAPTER IX

BANK NOTES AND PAPER MONEY

No survey of numismatics would be complete without some reference to paper money, although this aspect of the hobby has, until recently, been rather neglected. Paper money tends to be despised by many as something comparatively modern— and a poor substitute for specie at that. It comes as something of a surprise to most people to learn that paper money was in circulation at least a thousand years ago, so that, in terms of antiquity, it can claim a place alongside coins and medals.

Appropriately enough, paper money originated in China where paper itself was invented. The earliest form of paper money was produced sometime between 650 and 800 A.D. during the T'ang dynasty. At that period the coinage of China was bronze, and large quantities of it were needed even for relatively small transactions. This was not only inconvenient on account of its weight, but rather insecure. The cumbrous wagons used to convey these coins from one part of the country to the other were prone to ambush by bandits and it was in an attempt to defeat highway robbers that the Chinese merchants devised *fei-chen*, literally 'flying-money', consisting of paper drafts negotiable in bronze currency. These drafts were not authorised paper money in the modern sense but indubitably they paved the way for the paper money introduced by the Sung dynasty about A.D. 1000. These notes were redeemable in coin and quickly gained acceptance. Unfortunately the number of banks proliferated (there were no fewer than sixteen in the Szechuen Province alone) and they were tempted all too readily into issuing more and more notes without the funds or assets to back them. These notes, known as *djau-dze* (exchangeable money) soon lost the confidence of the populace, where-upon the Government began issuing *quei-dze* (citadel money) which, in turn, was over-issued and led to an inflation which contributed in no small measure to the downfall of the Sung dynasty in 1278.

Their successors, the Yuan dynasty (1260–1368), also issued far too much paper money. Before the end of the Mongol occupation of China this paper money had been reduced to worthlessness. A few examples of these very large and imposing notes have survived to this day, but rather more plentiful are the notes produced by the Ming dynasty (1368–1644). They were made from the bark of the mulberry tree and printed from wooden blocks. Marco Polo describes in some detail the paper money of Cathay:

'All these pieces of paper money are issued with as much solemnity and authority as if they were of pure gold or silver; and on every piece a variety of officials, whose duty it is, to have to write their names, and to put their seals. And when all is prepared duly, the chief officer deputed by the Khan smears the seal entrusted to him with vermilion, and impresses it on the paper, so that the form of the seal remains printed upon it in red; the money is then authentic. And the Khan causes every year to be made such a vast quantity of this money which costs him nothing, that it must equal in amount all the treasure in the world. When any of those pieces of paper are spoilt—not that they are so very flimsy either—the owner carries them to the mint, and by paying three per cent on the value he gets new pieces in exchange.'

With the collapse of the Ming dynasty in 1644 the use of paper money fell into abeyance. Two centuries later, however, the economic crisis engendered by the Taiping Rebellion of 1854–9 led the Imperial Government to resurrect paper money as an easy way out of its financial difficulties. Since then the paper money of China has earned for itself an unenviable reputation reflecting the fragmentation of the country between different factions and war-lords. Thousands of different notes have been issued in the past century and as most of them rapidly depreciated in value to the point of utter worthlessness they make ideal material for the collector of limited means. Chinese paper money is still fairly plentiful and few items should cost more than a pound, while the majority of items can be picked up for a matter of shillings. Many of them are extremely colourful, being the products of some of the world's finest security printers and the subjects depicted on them are full of interest.

Paper money came into being in England at roughly the same time as it went into oblivion in China, in the mid-seventeenth century. It developed out of notes issued by the goldsmiths as receipts for valuables deposited by merchants in their vaults, but the first issue to be accepted as legal tender was the Exchequer Order made by the authority of Charles II in 1665. Following the almost accidental establishment of the Bank of England in 1694 bank-notes were issued for large denominations (originally £50, but gradually lesser denominations were produced). Notes for £1 were not introduced till 1797 and until 1914 were not issued by the Bank of England, though all the provincial banks produced them. The unscrupulous issue of notes in the provinces undoubtedly weakened public confidence in them and precipitated the collapse of so many of the smaller banks in the early decades of the nineteenth century. The Bank Act of 1844 imposed serious restrictions on the issue of notes and eventually this privilege was confined to the Bank of England alone. This did not apply to Scotland whose banks have continued to produce their own notes, although, with the tendency for banks to merge into large combines the number of different banknotes currently issued is small.

European paper money had its inception in 1661 when the Stockholms Banco issued *kreditivsedlar* (credit notes) in place of the rapidly depreciating copper currency. The idea of producing these notes originated with Johan Palmstruch, a Dutchman resident in Riga (then a Swedish dependency), who first proposed such an issue nine years earlier. His credit notes were the first bank notes in the modern sense and not like the previous receipts given by the goldsmiths and merchant bankers for specific deposits. They were current in the hand of the bearer and did not earn interest. Professor Eli F. Heckscher, the leading Swedish economist, has stated that 'the promissory notes created later in the same century by Scottish and English banks were of the same character and influenced future developments infinitely more; but Palmstruch was their forerunner.' None of the first issue of *kreditivsedlar* has survived and fewer than a dozen specimens of the series of 1662 and 1663 are now in existence, all in various museum collections. The issue of 1666, however, is much more plentiful, though this was the last to appear. These notes seem to have been readily accepted by Swedish merchants, being infinitely more convenient to handle than the cumbersome copper plates, but the Stockholm Bank succumbed to the temptation of over-issuing. As early as 1663 the Bank was unable to redeem its notes and two years later the Swedish government decided that they should be abolished. The last issue was for silver dalers, since copper went out of circulation in 1665–6.

ASSIGNATS AND MANDATS

As a Scot I have somewhat mixed feelings about my fellow countrymen who had such an important influence on the development of European banking in the seventeenth and eighteenth centuries. On the one hand there was William Patterson who was largely instrumental in founding the Bank of England in 1694 and the Bank of Scotland in 1695, and well deserves his position as the father of British banking. On the other hand there was John Law, who founded the first French bank, the Banque Generale, in 1716. Law, born in Edinburgh in 1671, had a meteoric career in Continental banking; he formed the French Mississippi Company of Louisiana in 1718 and speculation in its shares was equalled only by the British South Sea Company. Like the latter, the bubble burst in 1720, and Law (who by this time had been appointed Comptroller General of France) had to flee the country.

Though Law had the misfortune to be discredited during his own lifetime, one of his economic precepts survived him—to cause even greater chaos and misery in his adopted country. He had proposed a land currency equal to the value of the land

and to the value of actual coined money without being subject, as was coined money, to a fall in value. This system was adopted by the French government on the verge of the bankruptcy which precipitated the Revolution of 1789–92. *Assignats* were issued in 1789, their value backed by the land confiscated from the Church at the outset of the Revolution. Each note had a nominal value of 100 livres bearing interest at 5 per cent. A total of 4,000 million livres was put into circulation in the first issue alone. Within a year the interest had been reduced to 3 per cent and a subsequent issue of 800 million livres bore no interest at all. The output of paper money grew faster and faster; by mid-1794 a total of 8,000 millions had been issued, but within two years the amount in circulation had spiralled to 45,500 millions. The value of the *assignat* fell rapidly. Even the earlier issues were reckoned to be worth only 20 livres in coin for every 100 in paper. By 1793 the depreciation had reached 97 per cent. The Directory fixed the value of the *assignats* at a thirtieth of their original value and then reduced it to a hundredth.

When the *assignats* sank to utter worthlessness the government had recourse to territorial money orders known as *mandats* which were put into circulation at the rate of one for 30 *assignats*. These notes were no more trusted than the *assignats* and actually depreciated more rapidly. In many cases the *mandats* were worthless before they could even get into circulation. The Directory finally gave up its experiments in paper money in 1797 when *assignats* and *mandats* were called in and exchanged for coin in the ratio of one livre coin for every 3,000 livres paper money. Genuine examples of these interesting mementoes of the French Revolution are plentiful and can still be picked up for as little as 5s. each but there are numerous counterfeits and bogus items which were produced to deceive collectors. A perusal of *The Assignats*, published by S. E. Harris in 1930, will enable the student to differentiate the genuine from the fraudulent notes.

NOTGELD

France's financial troubles of 1790–7 were as nothing compared with Germany's during and after the First World War. The value of the mark fell gradually in the latter part of the war and an ominous indication of the economic disaster to come was the disappearance of coins—not only gold and silver but even copper—from circulation. The monetary crisis, imminent for so long, struck suddenly at the end of 1921 when the mark plunged in value to a thousandth of its 1918 value. The Reichsbank's highest denomination banknote prior to this had been the 1,000 mark note of 1910; in January 1922 it was found necessary to issue 10,000 mark notes and within ten months 50,000 mark notes had to be released. On 1st February, 1923, a 100,000 mark note went into circulation, followed within three weeks by a million mark note. The following summary of the higher denominations and their dates of issue will give some idea of the astonishing inflation which overtook Germany from the summer of 1923 to the spring of 1924:

1923	1st June	5,000,000 marks
	25th July	50,000,000 marks
	22nd August	100,000,000 marks
	1st September	500,000,000 marks
	5th September	1 milliard marks
	(milliard=American billion=1,000,000,000)	
	10th September	5 milliard marks
	15th September	10 milliard marks
	1st October	20 milliard marks
	10th October	50 milliard marks
	15th October	200 milliard marks
	26th October	500 milliard marks
	1st November	10 billion marks
	(billion=American trillion=1,000,000,000,000)	
1924	5th February	20 billion marks
	10th February	50 billion marks
	15th February	100 billion marks

Before the inflation came to an end early in 1924, when Germany repudiated her National Debt and started again with a clean slate, a new system of paper money, guaranteed by mortgage bonds funded in real estate, was introduced. These rentenmarks were secured by interest-bearing bonds into which they could be automatically converted. The government succeeded almost miraculously in floating a gold loan which gave it breathing space and enabled the work of stabilising the currency to be carried out successfully. The enormously high denomination Reichsbank notes of this period can often be purchased for a few shillings, although some of the last issues, which were quickly superseded by the rentenmark, are scarce and rather expensive nowadays.

The hyper-inflation of 1923–4 was preceded, however, by a period extending from 1914 to 1923 when the absence of coins from circulation necessitated the issue of paper money in quite small denominations. These notes were issued in every town and village in Germany, by factories and co-operatives and institutions. Collectors classify this **notgeld** (emergency money) into three main categories. **Small Notgeld** comprises low denomination notes (10, 25 and 50 pfennigs as a rule) which gradually replaced silver coins from 1914 onwards. The wartime issues are extremely elusive and highly prized, but the notes issued in 1921–2 are still very numerous and can be purchased for as little as a shilling each. As many as 45,000 different types of *Small Notgeld* have been recorded.

With the beginning of the post-war inflation the group of emergency paper money known to students as **Large Notgeld** (*First Series*) came into being. These notes are found in denominations of 1 to 50 marks and the majority of the 4,000 types recorded are dated 1918. The last category, known as *Large Notgeld* (*Second Series*) appeared in 1922–3 to fill the gap which even the prolific issues of the Reichsbank could not close at this time. Some 3,600 types appeared in 1922, but more than 60,000 in 1923.

Latterly another element influenced the *notgeld*. Great ingenuity and artistry was shown by the issuing authorities in making their notes as colourful and interesting as possible. Often they commemorated local events and honoured historic personages. Before long these notes, particularly those rendered obsolete or invalid by the rising inflation, were being avidly collected and many towns and cities pandered to the collectors by producing long pictorial sets. Special albums were manufactured by Schaubek and other leading stationers to house collections of *notgeld* and many a provincial *rathaus* or village *handelskammer* made a tidy profit from sales of their notes to collectors. This business rapidly got out of hand, until the Reichstag stepped in with an edict in September 1922 forbidding this practice.

Notgeld is rising rapidly in value these days as the number of paper money collectors increases. Not so long ago a collection amounting to several thousand notes would scarcely find a purchaser for £5—or less than a penny a note; but some idea of the interest now being shown in these curious pieces may be obtained from the fact that a collection amounting to 70,000 items fetched £130 at a Sotheby's sale in February 1968. *Notgeld* has probably brought more new recruits to the hobby of paper-money collecting than any other form and it is supported by a formidable amount of literature. Much of this is in German, embodying the prodigious research of Dr. Arnold Keller, the doyen of paper money collectors. Among his books, without which the student would be infinitely poorer, the following are particularly recommended:

> *Das Deutsche Notgeld von* 1914.
> *Deutsche Kleingeldscheine,* 1916–22.
> *Die Deutsche Grossgeldscheine von* 1918–21.
> *Das Notgeld der Inflation,* 1922.
> *Das Notgeld der Deutschen Inflation,* 1923 (in eight volumes).

To a lesser extent *notgeld* appeared in 1947–8 during the transition period preceding the currency reform. Dr. Keller has provided, in *Das Notgeld der Warungsreform,* an exhaustive catalogue of these emergency notes.

AMERICAN PAPER MONEY

America is the home of the oldest-established society catering specifically to paper money collectors and though its title, the Maryland Foreign Papermoney Club, suggests that its members

PLATE X

Token Coinage

1) England, George III; (2) Bank of Montreal; (3) Prince Edward Island;
4) Quebec; (5) Upper Canada; (6) England; (7) New Brunswick; (8) Palmer
'mailcoach halfpenny'; (9) Nova Scotia; (10, 12) Irish 10d. tokens; (11) England
penny token.

confine their interests to countries other than the United States, it is safe to say that Americans study and collect their own paper money to some extent. Perhaps because all United States banknotes issued since 1861 are still redeemable collectors have tended to shy away from them and concentrate on the issues of other countries and other banks which, since they are no longer valid, have little or no monetary value and thus form the ideal basis for a collection.

Nevertheless American paper money has a long and fascinating history which has attracted many devotees. The paper money of the country dates from the colonial period and Massachusetts had the doubtful honour of issuing the first notes as long ago as 1690. Altogether some 252 separate issues were produced by the thirteen American colonies, while over the border in French Canada a shortage of specie led to the use of playing cards endorsed and stamped on their backs in various denominations. Whole cards, half cards and even smaller fractions of cards were in circulation for more than seventy years in the eighteenth century. The Canadian playing-card notes are extremely scarce, but a few of the American colonial notes can still be purchased for less than a pound.

During the Revolutionary War (1776–83) the Continental Congress of Philadelphia authorised paper money to defray the costs of throwing out the British. Continental dollars proliferated so rapidly (with a corresponding depreciation) that within four years the real value of the paper dollar had sunk to a fortieth of its nominal value. Although the worthlessness of Continental notes became proverbial at the time of their circulation they have since acquired considerable historical and political interest. The earliest issues were signed by members of the Congress and these are highly sought after on account of the autographs they bear. Many of them bear political slogans such as 'A lesson to arbitrary Kings and wicked ministers' while others contain references to the conditions under which they were issued. Some were produced by the states in order to pay their troops and bore statements to that effect with the names of individual soldiers inserted. These notes bore interest which, in turn, was met by further issues of notes promising that the sum would be paid 'at or before the end of one year after the expiration of the present war.'

In the early years of the nineteenth century there were many ephemeral banks in the United States which flourished perhaps for a year or two before crashing. The notes of these 'broken banks' are often beautifully engraved and full of historical and topographical interest, yet can be purchased for a few dollars at most.

The Civil War of 1861–5 was an interesting period in the annals of American paper money. The Confederacy issued paper money in denominations up to $100 and very handsome they were too. But since the Rebels lost the war their banknotes were repudiated by the Federal government and for many years Confederate paper money was regarded as something of a joke. Now, however, these attractive notes are beginning to rise slowly in value. To some extent their desirability has been heightened by the growth of a general interest in the Confederacy and anything pertaining to it. It has even been worth someone's time and trouble to produce quite passable counterfeits of these notes.

Inflation did not hit the North to the same extent but the shortage of specie was serious none the less. The previous chapter contains a reference to the earliest expedient adopted— the encased postage stamps; but the Federal authorities themselves took hold of the idea and projected it further. In August 1862 they produced the first issue of postage currency, consisting of 5, 10, 25 and 50c. denominations which could be redeemed at post offices for stamps of the equivalent value. The connection with stamps was strengthened by the fact that the earliest issues had reproductions of stamps engraved on them—five 5 cent stamps on the 25c. notes and five 10 cent stamps on the half dollar note. The allusion to postage stamps was taken a stage further by perforating the notes in the manner of stamps, though this unnecessary embellishment was soon done away with. The perforated notes are the rarest and now fetch up to $10 for the commonest denomination. Variations in the inscription and printer's imprint also affect the value to a large extent. The pretence of postage stamps was dropped in 1863 when small notes in denominations from 3c. to 50c. were issued as 'fractional currency'. The pictures of stamps were replaced by handsome portraits of George Washington but the inscription contained the phrase 'Receivable for all U.S. stamps,' so some connection with philately, albeit a tenuous one, was retained.

All issues of the United States, from the commencement of the Civil War onward, can still be redeemed at their face value at least (while some of them, bearing compound interest, are now worth a great deal more). Consequently all but the wealthiest collectors are deterred from studying them to any extent. Robert Friedberg's *Catalogue of United States Paper Money* lists all the notes, up to the highest denomination ($10,000), giving the would-be collector some idea of the formidable task which lies ahead. Some of these notes are extremely rare and in a few cases no specimens are believed to be unredeemed in the hands of collectors. Other books of interest to the American money enthusiast are William P. Donlon's *Priced Catalogue of U.S. Small Size Paper Money* (dealing with the small dollar bills issued since 1928) and *A Guidebook of U.S. Fractional Currency* by Matt Rothert, covering all the fractional issues from the Civil War and Reconstruction period (1862–76). The South is amply covered by *Confederate and Southern States Currency* by G. C. and C. L. Crisewell.

MILITARY NOTES

Bismarck is credited with having said that three things were required in order to fight a successful war—money, money and money. It has been seen that paper money usually proliferated in time of war as desperate governments sought ways and means of raising the necessary capital. The Bank of England issued no pound notes after 1825 till the outbreak of the First World War, when an emergency issue of £1 and 10s. was hurriedly introduced by the Treasury. The Bank Charter Act of 1844 was suspended, enabling banks to issue notes which were not backed by gold. The 'currency notes' of 1914 (often termed 'Bradburys', after John Bradbury whose signature they bear) were hastily printed by Waterlow and Sons, the stamp printers, and the paper used at first was in fact that normally used for postage stamps, bearing an overall watermark of small royal monograms. A 5s. note was also printed but never circulated, while a 2s. 6d. note was contemplated in October 1918, but the need for such a denomination receded with the end of the war a month later.

Paper money has had a more direct connection with wars, however. During the Boer War both sides had recourse to emergency issues of paper money. Notes in denominations of £1, 10s., 3s., 2s., and 1s. were issued in Mafeking between January and March 1900 while that town was under siege. Colonel Baden-Powell, commanding the defenders, enlisted the aid of Mr. R. Urry of the Standard Bank and arranged for the release of 'vouchers' for the three lowest denominations. These were strictly utilitarian, being printed entirely in letter-press. The main inscription read 'This voucher is Good for the sum of — And will be exchanged for coin at the MAFEKING BRANCH of the STANDARD BANK on the resumption of Civil Law.' The vouchers bore the signature of Captain H. Greener, Chief Paymaster of the Mafeking garrison.

The 10s. and £1 appeared in March and were much more ornate, not to say artistic, being designed by Baden-Powell himself. Later he described the rough-and-ready method used to produce the 10s. note: 'We tried various dodges, drew a design on copper, bit it out with acid alright, but could not get sufficient pressure to print it, though we tried it out through a mangle. Then we cut a croquet mallet in half and made a wood-cut.' The £1 was produced, like the distinctive Mafeking stamps, by photography using the ferro-prussiate process. Apart from the basic set of notes there are prominent varieties. The serial numbers on the 1s. and 2s. notes were preceded by the letters A (January) or B (February) and the first printing of the 10s. note contained the spelling error—'Commaning' instead of 'Commanding'. It is not known for certain how many of each denomination were issued. Several thousands of the lower denominations were put into circulation but it is believed that fewer than 700 of the £1 were issued and these are now very rare. As happens in so many other fields of paper money, non-numismatic interest (from Boy Scouts and devotees of Baden-Powell) has served to raise the price of Mafeking siege-notes considerably.

Far more plentiful are the notes printed by the Japanese during the Second World War for use in territories which they occupied in the Far East. Huge quantities of unissued notes fell into Allied hands at the end of the war and many a collector was introduced to the hobby by means of these notes. Invasion or Occupation money was produced by the United States, Britain, France, Russia, Germany and Italy as well as Japan during that war. Many veterans of the Normandy landings for example, will remember the small notes which were produced in 1944 for use in France as the Germans were pushed back.

Paper money was also issued by guerillas and partisans, ranging from the Polish underground forces to the Philippine freedom fighters. An unusual by-product of the war was the appearance of Yugoslav banknotes overprinted '*Verificato*' by the Italians, after the latter discovered that Montenegrin peasants were spending looted banknotes left behind by retreating Yugoslav Government officials. The notes thus overprinted were those held by the State Bank in Cetinje and all unoverprinted notes were promptly declared invalid.

Paper money was produced by and for the inmates of prisoner-of-war and concentration camps. The notes from Theresienstadt and the Lodz Ghetto are poignant and pathetic relics of the attempts at normal life within some of the 'restricted areas' set up by the Nazis for the victims of their persecution. Polish troops captured by the Germans in 1939 spent almost six years in P.O.W. camps and some of these huge detention centres, with inmates numbering many thousands, had their own 'banknotes' (as well as stamps). Examples of these notes are generally scarce and very seldom found in other than worn condition.

Even in peacetime paper money has been produced for the use of military personnel. American 'scrip' (Military Payment Certificates) and British 'baffs' (from the initial letters of British Armed Forces Vouchers) have been used in many postwar theatres of operations, from Germany and Japan to Egypt and Cyprus.

Literature on the subject of military paper money is more than ample. Japan's military currency in three wars (Russo-Japanese, 1904–5, and the two World Wars) is covered in great detail by Kugahara's catalogue (in Japanese, with an English synopsis), while the 1941–5 period is specifically dealt with in *Japanese Invasion Money* by A. R. Slabaugh. Mr. Slabaugh is also the author of *Prisoner of War Monies and Medals* which treats extensively of currency (both paper and token) and medals used in P.O.W., concentration and displaced persons' camps from the eighteenth century to the present day. The standard works on the Second World War are *Catalogo della Carta-Moneta d'Occupazione e di Liberazione della II Guerra Mondiale* by Dr. Gaston Sollner, and Raymond Toy's *World War Two Military Currency*.

Paper money was extensively produced by the various factions in Mexico during the revolution of 1913–17; more than a thousand different varieties have been recorded from this turbulent period, issued by states, districts, banks and military authorities. These colourful notes are very popular in the United States and consequently many of them are rather expensive, but some of the commoner notes can still be picked up for less than a dollar. Paper money was issued by authority of Lajos Kossuth during Hungary's abortive fight for freedom in 1848 and after the rising was put down Kossuth and his supporters fled to the United States where they raised funds by issuing bonds and certificates. The Fenians sought to finance their terrorist activities in Ireland, Britain and Canada during the same period by the issue of similar bonds. Both issues were well engraved, handsome mementoes of the struggles of the Hungarians and the Irish for their independence—and now greatly prized by collectors of these nationalities.

COMMEMORATIVE NOTES

Apart from many issues of *Notgeld*, which honoured famous persons and events, paper money of a commemorative nature has been infrequent. Indeed, many collectors believe that the dollar note produced by Canada in 1967 to mark the centenary of the Confederation was the first government-issued commemorative note. There have, in fact, been several notes in earlier times, but the Canadian dollar introduced a new concept—a commemorative note which was not intended for circulation (although regarded as legal tender). This note bore the dates '1867–1967' in place of the usual serial numbers. Collectors could obtain specimens of this note from the headquarters of the Bank of Ottawa in Ontario for $1.35, the extra amount covering registration and postage. Centennial banknotes, with serial numbers, were circulated normally during 1967 in place of the ordinary dollar note (issued since 1954) which was suspended for the year.

Apart from the Canadian centennial dollar note, commemorative banknotes have been confined to a few issues from other parts of the American continent. The earliest of these consisted of 1 and 2 gourdes notes issued by the republic of Haiti in 1904 to commemorate the centenary of Haitian independence. They portrayed respectively the patriots Jean-Jacques Dessalines and Nord Alexis. Six years later Mexico's Banco Minero released 5 and 10 peso notes in honour of the centenary of independence. Other issues have included Canada's Silver Jubilee 25 dollar note of 1935, Colombia's peso note for the quatercentenary of Bogota (1938), Cuba's peso note honouring the birth centenary of José Marti (1953), Dominica's 20 peso note of 1955 marking the jubilee of the Trujillo era and Venezuela's 5 bolivares note marking the quatercentenary of Caracas (1967).

COUNTERFEITS

Paper money has been forged on many occasions for many reasons and examples of counterfeit notes are of great interest to the collector. Apart from their comparative rarity (since most of them would be impounded and destroyed by the authorities) they invariably tell a story, and the more colourful the background history of a counterfeit the more its value is enhanced. The forgery of paper money in medieval China became such a serious matter that the government took the novel, if desperate, step of rounding up the most skilful of the forgers and appointing them to official posts in the Imperial Mint.

Counterfeiting in England was at one time punishable by

death, and later by transportation. The confidence-men of the eighteenth and early nineteenth centuries preyed on a gullible and barely literate populace by producing 'skit-notes' which bore reasonable imitations of contemporary notes. Parodies would be a better word since the counterfeiter cunningly altered the inscription and instead of promising to pay the bearer five pounds, for example, merely promised to pay five *pence*. These notes easily changed hands at markets and fairs and must have been quite numerous at one time, but they are very scarce nowadays.

The most notorious—and best-executed—counterfeits were those produced by various governments in an attempt to discredit their enemies. In the early 1920s the Horthy régime in Hungary was responsible for forging contemporary French banknotes as retaliation against the Treaty of Trianon. During the Second World War the Germans successfully forged Bank of England £5 notes and could have disrupted the British economy very gravely had these notes had a wide circulation. One man who suffered from these counterfeits was the Albanian valet to the British Ambassador in Ankara, Turkey. Code-named 'Figaro', he was paid in counterfeit fivers by the Nazis for spying on his master and micro-filming secret Foreign Office documents.

It is important to note that many countries, including the United States and Britain, have stringent regulations concerning the possession of counterfeits of notes which are still legal tender and this has somewhat militated against their popularity with collectors.

CONDITION

In general, the terms used to describe the condition of coins and medals are also applied to paper money, although the self-explanatory word 'crisp' will sometimes be found in descriptions of notes in that state of pristine freshness in which they left the printing-presses. 'EF' would apply to a note which was perfect in every respect but for a slight crease on one or two corners. 'Fine' would describe a note which had been folded, but was otherwise in reasonably uncirculated condition. 'Good' would indicate a piece bearing obvious signs of circulation but still good enough to keep in the collection. The other numismatic grades—'B.Unc.', 'V.F.' and so forth—will also be found to describe paper money, while the lower grades, such as Fair, Poor and Mediocre, are applied to items which are torn, badly creased or rubbed on the surface.

But while coin collectors despise the poorer grades, paper money enthusiasts are often content to include in their collections notes in relatively poor condition, even items which have been torn in half. This is due not so much to lower standards or a general lack of fastidiousness on the part of paper money collectors, as to the fact that many notes just do not exist in better condition. Since paper money collecting is essentially a twentieth-century hobby, receiving its main impetus after the German inflation period, it follows that very few of the earlier notes were obtained purely for collections. On the contrary, the majority of the earlier notes only came into the hands of collectors after a long and honourable life in everyday circulation. Consequently, bearing in mind that even high quality rag paper is not so durable as the metal used in coinage, it can scarcely be wondered at that collectors have often to accept notes in very poor condition.

From this it follows that the paper money collector has his own standards regarding the ethics of repairing a damaged item. It is interesting to note that, in the comparable hobby of philately, collectors regard a repaired stamp with horror and disgust and instinctively reject it, but the paper money collector will quite happily re-unite the scattered pieces of a banknote with adhesive tape or completely laminate the note in silk. Actually the difference between philatelists and paper money collectors is only one of degree and the passage of time will tend to lessen this difference. The very early philatelists were not very fastidious and many of the greatest rarities (the Hawaiian 'Missionaries' are an obvious example) have only survived in heavily repaired condition. Where a note is readily obtainable (e.g. a current issue) the collector will be satisfied with nothing less than crisp condition and, generally speaking, modern notes are not collected in grades below Good. The condition of notes has some bearing on their value, though the differential between the various grades is not as great as would be found in coins and medals. This is a rapidly expanding branch of numismatics, still comparatively in its infancy, and the next ten years will see a great many changes in values, both for individial issues and for different grades of condition. At the moment it is still possible to buy packets of 100 different *Notgeld* for £1 and many demonetised banknotes can be picked up for a shilling or less. But this happy state of affairs is disappearing as stocks of the commoner items vanish into more and more collections.

A few words on the care of paper money will not be out of place at this juncture. Bad creases can usually be improved by ironing out the note between sheets of blotting paper. Small repairs can be effected with the gummed tissue paper used to repair sheet music. Adhesive tapes such as Scotch Tape and Sellotape are not advisable since the sticky substance will discolour notes eventually and also has a distressing tendency to ooze out from the side of the tape, causing the note to stick to anything else with which it comes in contact. Badly damaged notes can be laminated in silk which is almost invisible and which greatly strengthens even the most fragile of pieces. The housing of a paper money collection presents little problems these days since there are several excellent albums on the market. The 'Rodney', 'Cumberland' and 'Collecta' albums manufactured in Britain contain a number of clear acetate envelopes secured in a stout binder by a peg or ring system. These albums were manufactured primarily for philatelists who wished to store envelopes, first day covers and postcards, but they are even more suitable for banknotes, where it is usually desirable to display both sides of the notes. Stamp or photograph albums are also popular, with photographic corners or stamp hinges used to hold the notes in place, but this system has the disadvantage that the back of the notes cannot be seen.

*   *   *   *   *

There are several useful introductory works on the subject of paper money. *The History of Paper Money* by Albert Pick traces the development of paper money from China to modern times, with emphasis on nineteenth-century Europe. Fred Reinfeld's *Story of Paper Money* provides a comprehensive history with a strong bias towards American issues and gives a rough indication of market values. George Sten's *Encyclopaedia of World Paper Money* is particularly useful for identifying notes by country, place or institution of issue, with copious cross-references. *World Paper Money Collection* by John E. Sandrock lists over 2,500 different notes and is revised periodically to bring it up to date. Dr. Arnold Keller is currently engaged in the compilation of a catalogue entitled *Paper Money of the World* which aims at standardising and collating all the available information on modern notes. Colin Narbeth's *Encyclopaedia of Paper Money* is the most up-to-date work on the subject. The first volume of George Sten's *Banknotes of the World* has recently been published, covering Aden to China in some detail. The rest of the world will be dealt with in another three volumes which Mr. Sten hopes to publish within the next few years.

The premier society catering to the currency collector is the Maryland Foreign Paper Money Club founded in 1961. Its name belies its international character; although based in Baltimore it has members in every part of the world including the Soviet Union and Communist China. Contact between members is maintained through the medium of *The Currency Collector*, the club's quarterly bulletin. Details of membership are available from the Secretary, 701 Hammonds Lane, Baltimore, Md 21225, U.S.A. The largest club is probably the Society of Paper Money Collectors, with several thousand members, mainly engaged in studying United States Currency.

In 1964 the International Banknote Society was founded and has a large membership, spread all over the globe. Its quarterly bulletin is available from Colin Narbeth, Mayfield Road, Walton-on-the-Naze, England and the annual subscription is a guinea ($3). Articles on all aspects of paper money are increasingly frequent in the general numismatic periodicals listed in Chapter V. In addition the Journal of the Essay-Proof Society of America deals with material ancillary to the actual issue of paper money, such as artist's sketches, proofs and 'specimen' items. This society is devoted to a rather specialised aspect of paper money which is, as yet, little regarded. As interest in proofs and specimens connected with postage stamp production is increasing, so also an interest in related material for banknotes and paper money will inevitably develop and already such recherché pieces as engraver's die proofs fetch comparatively high prices.

CHAPTER X

NUMISMATIC FASHIONS

T HE NEWCOMER to numismatics may have had his interest aroused initially by a handful of coins tucked away in a drawer, relics of holidays or business trips abroad, but he will very quickly lose interest unless his collecting follows some pattern. Bearing in mind the countless thousands of main-type coins issued in the past 27 centuries, not to mention the infinite variety of date, mint and die sub-types, the budding numismatist may be perplexed. Moreover, the would-be collector may feel that he has taken up the hobby too late and be unable to afford all but the most recent items. The aim of this chapter is to examine the various fields of coins and assess the possibilities which exist even at this late date.

It would be rash of me, however, to attempt to advise the collector of the investment potential of any particular field or emphasise those fields which would seem to have the brightest future. A few vague generalisations would obviously be insufficient, but if a particular field was advised the adviser risks his reputation. Moreover such advice, if widely publicised, might well cause an artificial rise in value which in the short term would seem to justify the prophetic abilities of the adviser, but in the long run would be liable to slump as the speculators unloaded their holdings.

Hindsight is easily acquired; looking back on the past twenty years anyone can tell you what you should have bought in 1948 or even 1958 and, indeed, they could hardly have gone wrong since the vast increase in the number of collectors has resulted in an inevitable rise in value in all sectors of numismatics. Yet, it seems that values have increased in some areas more than in others and even now there are aspects of coins which are neglected by the majority of collectors and are consequently undervalued. It is in these fields that the shrewd beginner can establish himself now and have reasonable hopes of seeing his investment mature handsomely.

GREEK AND ROMAN COINS

At first sight it would seem that the numismatist who intends to take up any of the classical series must have a very large purse. It is true that Greek and Roman gold is now largely beyond the reach of most collectors but there is still plenty of scope in the silver and bronze issues. Many silver didrachms and tetradrachms from the fourth century B.C. onwards can still be purchased for under £25 while the equivalent silver denarii of the Roman Imperial period should still be available at prices ranging from 25s. to £10.

Roman bronze coinage, with its vast range of portraits and mythological subjects, offers great opportunities to the collector willing to study the language and the history behind the various issues. Even now it should not be impossible to assemble a fairly comprehensive collection of Roman bronze illustrating the rise and fall of the Empire, from the handsome dupondii of Julius Caesar to the aptly named minimissimi which vividly recall the inflation which overtook the Empire towards the end of its life. Many of these coins can still be bought for a few shillings.

ANGLO-SAXON COINS

Collectors in the English-speaking world regard the Anglo-Saxon series as the forerunners of modern British coinage but in spite of this they have been largely neglected. They are more or less the preserve of antiquaries, museum curators and scholars, and numismatists in general have tended to shy away from them, perhaps through fear that they are so old that they must therefore be very expensive, or perhaps through a lack of knowledge of the language or abbreviations found on these coins. Yet these silver pennies have an indefinable charm which grows on anyone who begins to take an interest in them. Although portraiture on these coins is crude rather than realistic, the inscriptions make up for this in the interest they hold for the local historian. Silver pennies were minted all over England from the eighth century onward, in numerous mints ranging from Cornwall to East Anglia, from Northumberland to Kent, by authority of kings, princes and bishops.

Lack of interest has been engendered by a general lack of knowledge of these coins. But in recent years this has been amply remedied by Michael Dolley's *Anglo-Saxon Pennies* which forms a succinct introduction to the subject. More detailed information will be found in the first volume of North's *Hammered Coins*. Already the value of silver pennies is beginning to rise as a comparison of the prices listed in various editions of Seaby's *Catalogue* will reveal. Items which could be obtained for less than 10s. four years ago are now fetching up to £5 each and the average increase in value has been 40% each year. Admittedly many of the earlier pieces, and those from some of the smaller mints, are extremely scarce and correspondingly expensive, but it is still possible to buy pennies of King Edward the Confessor for less than £10 and pennies of Cnut for £25.

ANGLO-NORMAN COINS

The hammered coinage of England after the accession of William the Conqueror followed the same pattern as its predecessors but has always been more popular with numismatists and is consequently more expensive. Nevertheless, there are many opportunities for the newcomer. Silver pennies from the commoner mints such as Canterbury and Winchester can be purchased for £5 to £10 depending on the reign, though minor varieties such as coins struck by the semi-independent Earls of Northumberland are now approaching the £100 mark, even in F condition.

ANGLO-GALLIC COINS

This interesting aspect of British numismatics is almost entirely neglected in Britain, though interest is much keener on the Continent where prices tend to be much higher. The coins in this category were struck by the authority of kings of England

from Henry II (1154–89) to Henry VI (1422–71) for circulation
in Normandy, Aquitaine and other districts of which they were
at various times the feudal overlords, and culminated in the
regal issues of the latter king after he had succeeded Charles VI
as King of France in 1429. In general the gold coins of this
period are very expensive, though *saluts d'or* of Henry VI can
still be purchased for upwards of £80, depending on the mint
which issued them. The silver coinage, however, is relatively
cheap, ranging from a pound or two for the deniers of Richard
Coeur de Lion to £15 for an average specimen of the demi-gros
of the Black Prince. The various mints were never as numerous
as those operating in contemporary England, but there is
sufficient variety to occupy the life-long student. The only work
covering the entire field is L. M. Hewlett's *Anglo-Gallic Coins*
published in 1920 and long out of print. Were this to be
republished, the increase in collector interest would certainly be
reflected in an upsurge in values. As it is, the sale of Anglo-
Gallic coins at Glendining's in November 1967 established
many new records for the prices obtained, not only for the gold
coins but for the silver series also.

TUDOR AND STUART COINS

This period spans the two centuries from the accession of
Henry VII (1485), to the introduction of milled coinage in the
reign of Charles II (*c.* 1662). By now portraiture had improved
enormously and was to culminate, at the end of the period, in
the sensitive work of the Simons. For aesthetic reasons, therefore, the coins of the Tudors and Stuarts have long been
fashionable with numismatists and it is difficult to make a
collection covering this period as a whole without a large outlay.
Within the vast field, however, there are certain aspects which
can be concentrated on. The Civil War is one which is already
catching the attention of collectors who study the outputs of the
Tower Mint on one side and the often handsome coins of the
Aberystwyth, Oxford and Shrewsbury mints on the other.
Prices range from a pound or so, for the commoner pennies
minted in London by royal authority before the war broke out,
to £100 for the rarer pieces from the Royalist mints. Parlia-

PLATE XI

TOKENS

(1–4) 'Model' coins; (5, 7) France, Chamber of Commerce; (6) United States, Civil War token; (8) France, trader's token; (9) 'Spade Guinea' counter; (10) Belgium, tram-token; (11–13) brass counters; (14–16) Scottish communion tokens.

mentary issues and the subsequent coins of the Commonwealth are generally much cheaper.

BRITISH MILLED COINS

There are few opportunities left for the newcomer in the milled coinage of Britain from the end of the seventeenth century onwards. Good advice is to restrict one's interests to a particular denomination and follow it through its evolution from the reign of Charles II to the present day. The sixpence is an excellent coin to study in this respect. The handsome sixpences of Charles II can still be purchased in VF condition for about £10, though some dates command quite a premium. The sixpences of James II are relatively scarce and even specimens in F condition will cost £12 to £15 today, when they can be found.

There has not been much movement in the prices of William and Mary sixpences in the past year; they are fairly plentiful and range in price from about £1 to £5, with the rare 'plumes' and 'roses' types of 1699 fetching £15 to £25. The Queen Anne coins show a surprising amount of variety for such a short reign (1702–14). Those inscribed VIGO (1703) minted from silver captured from the Spaniards, are eagerly sought after and now go for about £8 to £10. During 1707 the Union of Scotland and England was effected and that year witnessed two styles of design in the coinage. The sixpences after 1707 are relatively common and can be picked up in VF condition for under £5. George I pieces are rather elusive, but no difficulty should be experienced with the later Georges. As the coins of later reigns become more plentiful, condition becomes very much more important.

Broadly speaking the same pattern holds good for the other denominations in silver though there is a notable shortage of fine quality halfcrowns these days, with a consequent effect on the price asked. A relatively modern coin which is worth studying in detail is the florin. Introduced in 1849 (patterns exist dated 1848), it was Britain's first essay in decimalisation and bore the significant inscription 'ONE TENTH OF A POUND'. Apart from 1854 and 1927, when few florins were minted, a complete run from 1849 to 1967 should not present too great a problem, but if one aims at specimens in the best possible condition the task will be much more difficult, even though rewarding in the long run.

CROWNS

The earliest English crowns were gold coins, minted in 1526 by authority of Henry VIII, but the familiar large silver coin which we associate with this denomination appeared in the reign of his son Edward VI and was designed as the English counterpart of the German thalers. The large surface has enabled artists over the past four centuries to produce some striking designs, the best-known being Pistrucci's *St. George and the Dragon*, used intermittently from 1818 to 1951. In the last hundred years, however, they have not been very popular on account of their size and their issue has tended to be more of a commemorative nature. In recent years crowns have been minted to mark the silver jubilee of George V (1935), the coronations of George VI (1937) and Queen Elizabeth (1953), the Festival of Britain (1951) and in memory of Sir Winston Churchill (1965).

Though unpopular in circulation, crowns are popular with collectors and they make an ideal subject for a world-wide collection. In recent years crowns have been issued by Bermuda, Gibraltar, Jamaica, Malawi, South Africa, New Zealand and Zambia among others and have attracted a great deal of attention. As a result the prices of some items have risen sharply —the Gibraltar proof crown of 1967 in silver, now valued at around £10, is a dramatic example.

Some idea of the scope of the crowns of the British world can be gained from Howard Linecar's *The Crown Pieces of Great Britain and the British Commonwealth* which lists all the main types with very few exceptions.

MAUNDY MONEY

Though not confined solely to Britain the Maundy Thursday ceremony of distributing money to the poor has special reference to Britain on account of the special coins minted for the occasion.

The ceremony derives its name and procedure from the *mandatum* of Our Lord to His Disciples on the day before he was crucified, the chief link being the washing of the feet. This ritual has changed over the years and developed into the distribution of food and clothing to a number of paupers; subsequently the food and clothing was transformed into a cash payment, and the washing of feet was dispensed with, though certain officials of the Royal Maundy ceremony are girt with towels to this day as a symbol of the former ritual.

Maundy pensioners are chosen 'from among those who apply to the Royal Almonry for assistance, preference being given to those who have formerly been householders paying rates and taxes and who have been employers of labour.' This ceremony dates back hundreds of years before the Welfare State was established to ensure that no one went without. The Royal Bounty was looked to, to take care of the deserving poor and the Royal Maundy is one of the few vestiges of this which has survived. At some date, lost in the mists of antiquity, the payment of the bounty was commuted to cash in the form of four silver coins—the penny, half groat (2d.), threepence and groat —totalling tenpence. A later development was to give each pensioner as many pence as the sovereign had years of age. The Royal Maundy was given to as many men and women. Thus this year (1968) the Queen distributed 41 pence to 41 men and 41 women. The coins were made up of four sets, with an extra penny thrown in, so that 328 sets were issued to pensioners this year, plus a number of sets given to officials connected with the ceremony.

It follows that Maundy money (the only silver coins minted in Britain since 1946) varies in value from year to year depending on the age of the sovereign. In addition, an unlimited quantity of Maundy money was minted each year until 1909, to satisfy the demand from collectors; so that Victorian and early Edwardian sets are commoner than the later issues. Nevertheless, considering the fact that Maundy money constitutes the world's scarcest regularly issued coinage, prices are still surprisingly reasonable. For £20 one may still hope to purchase sets from most years since Charles II. Even 'young head' Victoria sets of

1839–40 can be picked up for this sum, while sets from 1890–1901 are usually obtainable for half that amount. One of the most expensive of all Maundy sets is, in fact, the Elizabethan Coronation set of 1953 which currently sells around the £75 mark. This is one field of British coinage which seems bound for a hefty increase in the near future. The specialist dealer in this material is the aptly named Maundy Allen of Great Portland Street, London.

BRITISH COPPER COINS

When farthings were on the verge of demonetisation in 1956 a friend of mine purchased £1 worth from a local bank, for use as gaming counters. On looking through this huge accumulation of almost 1,000 coins he was astonished at the range of dates and the fine state of the majority of the pieces. He subsequently acquired several bags at a pound a time—and became an addicted numismatist as a result. The last farthing of all (1956) now fetches from 15s. to £1—a fantastic increase in value in twelve years. The value of some of the earlier dates in B. Unc. condition seems a little erratic at the moment, bearing little relation to the numbers minted. The copper farthings minted up to 1860 are not as popular for some reason as the bronze issues from 1860 onwards: compare the 1861 date (8 millions minted) which is now priced at £3, with the 1858 date (2 millions minted) which only rates £2 10s. The shrewd collector would do well to concentrate on the copper issues before their value rises commensurate with their true scarcity.

Pennies and halfpennies are not perhaps so glamorous as the humble farthing—familiarity breeds contempt—but there is plenty of interest to be found in them and the possibilities for the collector are well-nigh infinite. The minting of coins of these denominations was sporadic before the nineteenth century but their issue has been more or less continuous since 1797 and the past 170 years forms a convenient period for study.

The cartwheel pennies and twopences of the 1790s are hardly elegant, but the sheer novelty of their cumbrousness has ensured them a permanent place in the affections of numismatists. These large pieces now fetch up to £9 in EF condition and £2 in VF, but poorer specimens are fairly common. Because the metal used was very soft, these coins did not wear well and this accounts for the fact that so many of them are in worn condition with edge knocks and scratches, but it pays to look out for fine examples. The great size of these coins encouraged jewellers and smiths to fashion curiosity boxes out of them. One will occasionally find in junk shops, among the assortment of curios, a cartwheel twopence whose obverse unscrews to reveal a hollow interior. Inside lies a cartwheel penny which likewise unscrews to reveal a halfpenny. These items have no numismatic interest, but are highly regarded by collectors of by-gones.

COMMEMORATIVE COINS

The dual role of some Roman and Greek pieces, intended as commemorative coins valid for circulation as money, has already been mentioned but throughout the ages there have been many other examples of this sort. Nevertheless it would be true to say that the commemorative coin is essentially modern in concept, having its origins in the half-dollars produced in the United States between 1892 (Columbus Exposition) and 1954 (George Washington Carver). Altogether 48 half-dollars, one silver dollar and a quarter-dollar were produced during that period to commemorate various events of greater or lesser importance. Undoubtedly the practice got out of hand in the 1930s—no fewer than 16 half-dollars appeared in 1936 alone—and few commemorative coins have appeared in the United States since that time. The Kennedy half-dollar, though commemorating the late President, is not a commemorative coin in the true sense since it was introduced, albeit contrary to the normal American custom, as a replacement for the Franklin half-dollar and thus should be in use for about 25 years.

Most gold coins in the past thirty years are purely commemorative since gold has seldom circulated in the ordinary way since the First World War. Numismatists are debarred (in the United Kingdom at any rate) from collecting them unless they have the necessary authorisation to do so and consequently this is an area which is pretty stagnant just now. Having been

frustrated in this direction, collectors have been focusing their
attention on the other commemoratives, struck in silver or
cupro-nickel as a rule, and it would appear that governments
are now pandering to this by stepping up the output of such
pieces. It is significant that more than a quarter of all new
issues minted in the period June 1966–June 1967 were purely
commemorative in nature. Apart from the £5, £1 and 10s. gold
coins issued by Rhodesia to mark the first anniversary of
U.D.I. in November 1966, the other pieces (some 22 in all)
were struck in silver or cupro-nickel and were thus within the
financial range of most collectors. Indeed it has been estimated
that £15 would have secured them all, in the ordinary, non-
proof state at any rate—an outlay of little more than £1 a
month. Proofs, where they existed, would have cost much more
—about £60 altogether (or slightly over £1 a week). Because
the proofs were limited (to editions of 2,500 as a rule) they had
better prospects of rising in value and in fact have turned out to
be a sound investment so far.

The Gibraltar crown was minted in an edition of 250,000 in
cupro-nickel and 20,000 proofs in silver. The former normally
retailed in London at 10s. while the latter sold initially for
£3 10s. In spite of its relatively high mintage, however, the
proof was oversubscribed at the time of its release and those
specimens which got on to the retail market quickly climbed to
£8 and are still rising, though the rate of increase has levelled
off somewhat. The larger dealers, such as Spink and Seaby,
have a new issue service which guarantees their regular customers against missing out on any surprise issues which often
tend to be in short supply.

MODERN WORLD COINS

The newcomer to numismatics will have had copious advice
—in this book and in others—against trying to tackle too wide a
field. While it is a good tip to study a specific aspect of numismatics in depth, thereby forming a collection which has some
cohesion and an entity in itself, the beginner may find himself
frustrated because certain key dates or mint marks are
exceptionally scarce so that he is unable to achieve the desired

degree of completion. If only he had been collecting twenty—or even ten—years ago it would have been infinitely easier. Why not, therefore, start with a clean slate as it were and concentrate on coins as they are released from now onwards? As against the disadvantage of having a world-wide collection in no way specialised is the advantage of having cast the net as wide as possible so that while some coins will show little or no appreciation as the years go by, others will make rapid progress. Like unit trusts, world-wide collecting is a safe, if unspectacular, form of investment. Since it is virtually impossible in the world of coins and medals to predict which area is going to prove the best investment, it follows that a general collection of modern world coins is the surest way of investing one's money and hoping for at least a modest increase in value.

No one in their right mind would consider forming a collection of all the postage stamps issued throughout the world, since the annual output is now in excess of 6,000 items. Coins, on the other hand, are far less numerous and the total output of new issues in the period noted above was 93 coins. All of these could be purchased at the time of issue for a sum not exceeding £50, or about £1 a week. One can tailor this collection to suit one's pocket by taking or disregarding year-dates and mint-marks as one pleases. Brand new coins, purchased through a new issue service in uncirculated condition, should turn out to be a sound investment in the long run.

CASED SETS

The problem of housing coins (discussed at greater length in the next chapter) may be solved if one collects cased sets. These fall into several categories. At one extreme there are the sets of coins, often in proof state, which have been placed in velvet-lined leather cases of a sumptuousness in keeping with the de luxe coins themselves. Such cases are invariably manufactured for the government or mint issuing the coins and are often beautifully embossed with a coat of arms and suitable inscription. The case and the coins are inseparable as a collector's piece and, in fact, the coins should be disturbed from their setting as little as possible. Cased sets of this sort are highly prized by collectors and, although they are initially expensive to purchase, should show a better-than-average rate of increase in value over the years.

The second category of cased sets also consists of officially produced items, but the cases in this instance are much more utilitarian in composition, being produced in some form of plastic or acetate as a rule. One advantage of the plastic sets is that both obverse and reverse of the coins can be seen at the same time without any actual handling of the coins themselves. Unfortunately the plastic used is seldom chemically inert, with the result that coins contained in these cases often tend to become toned over the years. It is unwise, however, to remove the coins from their plastic case in order to prevent this toning. This patina does not diminish their value, whereas the original plastic case enhances it.

A good example of this is the plastic case containing the set of Elizabethan coins minted in 1953. These were freely available from banks at their face value of 7s. 4¾d., but after a slow rise during the 1950s and early 1960s began to increase sharply in value in the past three years, so that, at the time of writing, a 'plastic set' will fetch anything up to £15. Many of these cases have been broken up in the intervening years either to provide uncirculated specimens for year sets or, regrettably in the early years, because their owners tired of waiting for the sets to rise in value and merely broke them up in order to spend the coins! The result is that the plastic cased sets of 1953 are now quite scarce and the supply cannot keep up with the demand. Whether the new decimal sets in plastic cases will turn out to be such good property remains to be seen. There are more collectors in Britain today and the number of cases sold is bound to be proportionately higher. Nevertheless no collector can afford *not* to take the opportunity while they are still available to acquire one set at least.

The third category consists of sets made up and cased by numismatic dealers. This style of casing originated in the United States and is extremely popular there, where nearly all the modern coins are now sold in cases of one sort or another. In Britain the best known cases are those manufactured by

Sandhill which are widely used in the retail trade. They consist of slim plastic boxes containing cards punched with holes to take coins of certain sizes. The cards can be obtained annotated with brief captions such as year dates and denominations; and sometimes additional inscriptions, with data regarding the country of issue, are included. The value of such cased sets is less than the *official* cased sets, though they have the common advantage in reducing the handling of the coins themselves to the bare minimum. Empty Sandhill and other cases can be purchased from most dealers to enable collectors to build up their own sets. This is important to remember when buying cased sets, since not all sets are necessarily in B. Unc. condition.

Another recent development which might well be mentioned here is the roll or rouleau of coins, much favoured by investors who prefer their coins to come 'not single spies but in battalions.' It is not uncommon these days for certain dealers to sell rolls containing 50 or 100 coins, all of the same denomination and date, in B. Unc. condition as an investment. Presumably these rolls are then filed away and never looked at, until such times as the investor decides to unload his holdings on to the market. This situation, relatively new to numismatics, is analogous to the stamp collector's mania for buying new issues in complete sheets. Since rolls of coins are easier to look after it is to be presumed that this form of 'collecting' is bound to spread—but it can hardly be regarded as true numismatics. The pure numismatist has a hearty contempt for the roll collector (and his first cousin, who stores sealed bags of newly minted coins like the misers of old), but true collectors should be grateful to the investors since they are responsible for preserving in pristine condition a vast amount of newly released coins which might otherwise have got into circulation and suffered some deterioration in condition as a consequence. Judging by the number of 1965, 1966 and 1967 British coins of every denomination which are being salted away in rolls and bags at the moment it would seem likely that B. Unc. specimens will be fairly plentiful for many years to come.

Whether investment rolls will turn out to have been worth the effort and money expended on them is debatable, but since it is the 'in' thing to do there is no shortage of people busily engaged in this pastime and many dealers cater to it by advertising such rolls. At the time of writing, I note that rolls of 100 halfpennies dated 1959 and 1960 are currently selling for £11 and £8 10s. respectively. The former represents an increase of 500% per annum, but it should be pointed out that comparatively few people were bothering about salting away uncirculated rolls and bags ten years ago. It is unlikely that the coins of the past three years will appreciate so dramatically in value, even though 1967 is the last date to appear on them before they are replaced by decimal currency.

NORTH AMERICAN COINS

The coins of North America have been so popular in their own country for so many years that they now offer little scope for the beginner. There was a time not so long ago when the American collector, faced with high prices at home, could pick up reasonable quantities of cents, nickels, dimes, quarters and dollars by touring the dealers' shops in Britain and Europe. This happy position has vanished and the past decade has witnessed a steady drain of U.S. coins in all grades back to America. Consequently few dealers in Britain now carry large stocks of American material, and what they have is now as dear to buy here as it is on the other side of the Atlantic. This need not deter the would-be collector of Americana since current developments in U.S. coinage offer a fair measure of scope. The demise of the all-silver coins, and their replacement by the 'clad' coinage in the past two years, has stimulated a great deal of interest both inside and outside America.

The coins of Canada are in a similar position and in recent years have been eagerly taken up by collectors in the United States who, finding their own coins increasingly difficult to collect, have been turning to other fields near at hand. Logically Mexico is next on the list, but here the language barrier may have been sufficient in the past to deter large-scale collecting. This argument is unlikely to prevail much longer and already Mexican coins, particularly the handsome silver dollars, are becoming elusive in the better grades.

FOREIGN COINS

Excluding the new issues mentioned above there are several areas of foreign coins which still hold opportunities for the newcomer. In general, European coins since the end of the Second World War are still reasonably plentiful and are available at reasonable prices. There is relatively little demand for them in Britain and America though this seems likely to increase. The coins of most European countries are freely available, though there is an embargo on the export of material from certain Communist states.

The issues of Latin America are fairly popular with collectors in the United States, particularly the dollar-sized silver coins, such as the balboa of Panama, the sol of Peru, the old peso of Argentina and the quetzal of Guatemala. The market for such pieces is strong, but rather weaker for lesser denominations at present. This could be a fertile area for the collector starting now.

African coinage is a comparatively new field and, apart from the dirhems and dinars of the caliphates which circulated along the Mediterranean coast from Egypt to Morocco in the ninth century onwards, the coins of the modern African states date from 1833, when the copper token cent of Liberia appeared. In much of the continent the currencies of Britain, France, Spain and other European colonial powers circulated till fairly recently, so that indigenous coinage is of recent origin in most cases. Where distinctive coinage was struck for colonial possessions it is usually keenly collected. Particularly popular, for example, are the handsome hellers and rupees minted for use in the erstwhile German colonies in East and West Africa. The coinage of the Republic of South Africa is very highly regarded and the market is strong in all periods from the rixdalers of the Cape Dutch colony of the seventeenth century, through the coins of the Transvaal and the Orange Free State (including the famous and now excessively expensive 'veld-ponds' of the Boer War) to the crowns and lesser denominations minted by the Union, and now the rands and cents of the Republic.

Apart from the very recent issues, the newcomer has little hope of getting together a comprehensive collection for the minimum outlay. Uncirculated sets of the obsolete sterling currency have risen sharply in value over the past two years. On the other hand there seems to be plenty of scope for the collector who concentrates on the coins of the emergent African states, such as the Congo, the Sudan, Burundi and the monetary union of Equatorial Africa and Cameroun. Most of them have only appeared since the Second World War and it is still an easy matter to form complete collections of the regular issues, and even proofs present little problem.

Asia is an exceedingly complex area from the numismatic viewpoint since its coinage dates back to the dawn of history— it must be remembered that it was here that coins were first produced. The ancient coinage of India, Ceylon, Palestine, Asia Minor and China is not only rather hard to find nowadays, but deters most collectors on account of the language problems Representations of animals or humans being frowned on in the Moslem world, the medieval coinage of the caliphates tends to appear dull to the beginner, with its designs consisting almost entirely of inscriptions. These are often difficult for even the Arabic scholar to decipher on account of the stylised Cufic script used, often in a highly abbreviated form. Another factor militating against their popularity is the unfortunate existence of so many forgeries or completely bogus pieces, sold to tourists in the bazaars. Unless one develops a great familiarity with these coins, their inscriptions and styles from a study of museum collections and catalogues, it is as well to leave them alone.

COMMONWEALTH COINS

Many countries of the British Commonwealth used the coins of the mother country almost exclusively until recently and, indeed, certain territories still do, so that this is a fairly small field expanding rapidly and possessing a good investment potential.

It is important to note, however, that some colonies, which now use British coins, or have only recently begun using their own coins, have had money of their own in times past. Gibraltar is a case in point. In 1842 it had its own distinctive coins, bearing the sovereign's bust on the obverse and the castle and key emblem on the reverse. Since that date it has used British coinage exclusively, apart from the crown of 1967. Malta has used British coins since it was occupied in 1802, although the tiny third of a farthing coin was minted specifically for use in the island between 1844 and 1913 as a substitute for the copper grano. Before the British period, however, Malta had a long and distinguished series of coins struck by the authority of successive Grand Masters of the Knights of St. John. Apart from two commemorative crowns in the past decade Bermuda has always used British coins in modern times, but in the early seventeenth century produced the silver-washed copper coins known as 'Hogge Money' from the emblem of a wild pig found on their obverse. Genuine examples of these coins, in denominations of 1d., 3d., 6d., and 1s., are extremely rare. Some idea of the scope of colonial coinage may be gained by Captain Pridmore's *Coins of the British Commonwealth of Nations* or Howard Linecar's *British Commonwealth Coinage*.

Apart from Canada, whose coinage dates back to French colonial days, the dominions have begun to issue their own coins in comparatively recent times. Australia began issuing her own coins in 1901, New Zealand not until 1933 and Southern Rhodesia in 1934. Conversely, although Jamaica did not become politically independent till 1965, small denomination cupronickel coins (farthing to three halfpence) were in circulation as long ago as 1880. Cyprus has had its own coins since it came under British control in 1878 and these are now becoming very popular, especially with Continental collectors.

Also popular at the moment are the coins minted for use in the Ionian Islands between 1809 and 1863 when they were ruled by Britain. The first 1 and 2 obols are far scarcer than their mintage figures would suggest (8 and 4 million respectively). The first issue, however, was very unpopular with the islanders and of the 198 tons minted, 150 were subsequently returned to England for melting down. Mintage figures for the later issues are not known, a factor which tends to be in the collector's favour since some of the rarer items can still be picked up as unconsidered trifles.

Not part of the Commonwealth, but associated with it in

many respects, is the Republic of Ireland in which British coins circulate freely alongside the distinctive Irish series. The attractive pictorial coins first appeared forty years ago. Since then the eight denominations have changed in inscription (from 'Saorstát Eireann' to 'Eire' in 1939) and in composition (the 3d. and 6d. from pure nickel and the higher denominations from silver to cupro-nickel). Perhaps these changes are insufficient to maintain interest, but collectors are now beginning to realise that some dates are quite elusive. Moreover, the appearance of a ten shilling coin in 1966, portraying Padraic Pearse and commemorating the Jubilee of the Easter Rising, has helped to bring Irish coins into the limelight.

THALERS

The discovery of silver in the Joachimsthal region of Bohemia led to the minting of large silver coins by the Counts of Schlick in 1518. The 'Joachimsthalers', rapidly abbreviated to 'thalers' became popular all over the Holy Roman Empire, superseding the clumsy Tyrolese guldengroschen minted thirty years earlier. Every principality, duchy and free city of the Empire produced its own thalers at one time or another and altogether they amount to a formidable field. Their large size gave more scope to the designers and many of the early thalers are fascinating, with their elaborate coats of arms and attractively sculpted portraiture. The thaler spread beyond its native Germany, Austria and Hungary. It went to Spain, where i became the eight-real coin—the 'pieces of eight' of the buc caneers—and thence became adopted all over the America continent as the dollar (the dollar sign is a corruption of th figure eight and two vertical strokes used to denote the eight real coin). It spread to the Low Countries and Scandinavi where it became the daler, and to the Mediterranean where i was known as the tallero or escudo (from the shield depicted o it). The thaler in its many forms has survived even to this day though the only coin which closely retains the name is th talari of Ethiopia.

That Ethiopia should cling so steadfastly to this name is r accident, since it is in north-east Africa and Arabia that tim so far as the thaler is concerned, has stood still. At some date in the dim and distant past the handsome thalers of the Empress Maria Theresa of Austria, dated 1780, were introduced to the Middle East, where they gained an acceptance which has endured to this day. As a result the Maria Theresa thaler of 1780 has been minted regularly ever since, not only in Vienna, but by the Royal Mint and in many other mints as well. Numismatists have made a special study of this coin and its numerous die variants. Brilliant uncirculated specimens fresh from the mint, but still bearing the serene features of that long dead monarch, can be bought today for a few shillings and are now as popular with collectors as they are and were with the traders of the Red Sea area.

The thaler, as legal tender, came to the end of its career in 1872 when, following the establishment of the German Empire under the hegemony of Prussia, the mark of 100 pfennigs was introduced as the monetary unit. Ironically, one of the last thalers to be minted was the Victory Thaler of 1870-1 commemorating the Franco-Prussian War. In fact, if not in name, the thaler has survived in another guise. Even after the founding of the German Reich the individual states continued to mint their own higher denominations, the 2, 3 and 5 mark pieces. No fewer than 25 kingdoms, principalities, duchies and free cities struck their own large silver coins between 1873 and the First World War and many of these items were commemorative in nature.

In the period of the Weimar Republic and the Nazi régime the thaler was transformed into the numerous commemorative reichsmark coins, while the present Federal Republic has produced silver 5-deutschemark coins in commemoration of the Jurnberg Museum, Friedrich Schiller, Ludwig von Baden and Freiherr von Eichendorf. Many of the thalers of the nineteenth century and their successors can still be purchased for a pound or two, though the earlier pieces are more expensive.

In Austria the vereinsthalers of 1½ florins were minted between 1857 and 1865 for circulation throughout the States adhering to the Zollverein (Customs Union) agreed in the former year. The Seven Weeks War of 1866 brought to an end

Austria's supremacy over the south German states and with the creation of the Dual Monarchy of Austria-Hungary two years later the thaler ceased to be current. Nevertheless large silver coins in the size of the thaler have continued to appear, usually as commemoratives. The two-florin and five-kronen coins of the monarchy and the 25 schilling coins of the present republic are the lineal descendants of the thaler in Austria while, in Hungary, the five-korona and five-pengö coins of the pre-war period and the 10, 20 and 25 forint commemoratives of more recent years carry on the thaler tradition.

Austria's last coin actually designated as a thaler appeared in 1868 to mark the Third German Shooting Festival in Vienna. This reminds me of another important group of thaler-sized coins, the *Schutzenfestmünzen* of Switzerland. These attractive silver pieces were struck until just before the Second World War and were produced for distribution as prizes in cantonal and federal shooting festivals. Prior to the 1860s the mintages of these coins never exceeded 6,000 but in later years anything from 10,000 to 30,000 pieces were minted, so they can still be located without too much difficulty.

MISCELLANEOUS ITEMS

Principal among the 'odds and ends' of the numismatic world which are gaining in popularity with collectors are primitive currencies of various kinds. This is a relatively new field which still offers a great many opportunities to the newcomer since interest is nascent and the literature on the subject fairly limited. Shell discs from the Pacific, cowries from Africa and wampum from America form one group. Primitive metallic currency includes Chinese cash, manilla rings from Nigeria, the distinctive crosses from Katanga, the plate money of Sweden and the iron ingots of Ancient Britain. Primitive money presents its own problems, particularly of storage and display, since it ranges from the cakes of tea used in the Himalayas to the enormous circular stones favoured by affluent society on Yap Island in the Pacific. The inconvenience of primitive money has often deterred much numismatic interest in the past, but there are signs of a marked increase in interest lately.

PLATE XII

<small>BANKNOTES</small>

(1) Royal Bank of Scotland £1 portraying David Dale, the 18th-century manufacturer and philanthropist; (2) Germany: Inflation note of the Reichsbank, 1923,
for 10,000,000 marks.

In Victorian times it was fashionable to make jewellery out of coins by applying coloured enamel to different parts of their surface. Enamelled coins became popular for mounting on watch-chains, bracelets, cuff-links, ear-rings and brooches when the Jubilee series of coins appeared in 1887. The best enamelling was carried on in Birmingham by W. H. Probert and Edwin Steele during the last two decades of the nineteenth century. Coin-enamelling survived on the Continent as late as 1920 where the French jeweller Louis Elic Millenet specialised in this art. The coins most often found treated in this way are the crowns showing St. George and the Dragon, the Jubilee series bearing the royal coat of arms, the Peacock rupees of Burma and the early 5-franc pieces of France. Fine examples of enamelled coins can be picked up in jewellers shops and curio shops. Numismatic interest in enamelled coins was virtually non-existent until recently. In January 1967 F. J. Jeffery published a short article on this subject in *Coins and Medals*; more recently, a statement in *Coins, Medals and Currency* that enamelled coins were of no numismatic interest or value, had to be retracted following vigorous protests by readers to the contrary. Thus, yet another of the by-ways of the hobby is coming into prominence.

Numismatists are also beginning to take an interest in ancillary material such as coin-weights, coin-balances and money-boxes and competition for these items at auctions is keen. Not so long ago I purchased a sovereign pocket balance in a Welsh antique shop for 10s.; the same article sells in London for at least £5. Antique and junk shops and auction sales of Victoriana and 'bygones' are a fertile source of this material but, significantly, there is very much less of it to be found these days than even two years ago.

CHAPTER XI

THE CARE AND DISPOSAL OF COINS

ENOUGH has already been said about the importance of condition in affecting the value of coins and medals and by now the reader will be well aware of the fact that it is in his own interests to buy the finest material he can afford and not be content with second rate pieces which will not show as good a rate of appreciation. It is essential, however, that the collector should protect his investment and there is nothing more distressing than the sight of coins bought in F.D.C. or B. Unc. condition, which have been allowed to deteriorate through the ignorance of their owners. Edge knocks and finger prints are probably the commonest evidence of unintentional vandalism. Even less forgivable are these well-meaning individuals who think they are improving the appearance of their coins by giving them a periodic rub with metal polish. Such action can only result in the loss of the original lustre, or the protective patina of the years. Coins *can* be cleaned (as opposed to polished) but this is a task for the expert and should not be lightly undertaken.

The housing of a collection of coins and medals is also fraught with dangers. The cardinal sin is to leave one's treasures lying loose in a box or in a drawer where they can rub against each other. Admittedly some of my best purchases came from dealers' 'smelt trays' or junk boxes where they had lain unrecognised and grossly undervalued, but this would have been no excuse for me to have continued to treat them so cavalierly.

The traditional, if rather expensive, method of housing coins is the coin cabinet constructed of specially selected and seasoned timber. It is important that a timber such as mahogany or rosewood, virtually free of harmful acids or oils, should be used. Oak and cedar, on the other hand, should be avoided like the plague since they contain chemicals which attack metals. Coin cabinets contain a number of shallow wooden trays which are punched with circular holes of various diameters suitable for coins of all sizes. On the underside of each tray are smaller holes so that the coins may be pushed up gently with the finger to remove them. On no account should coins be prised out with the fingernails since even the slightest scratches will cut their value considerably. The disadvantages of these cabinets are their cost, which is high, and their cumbrousness—and in these days of small houses space is an important consideration. Nevertheless cabinets are popular since they display coins with a dignity lacking in other methods. Until recently it was impossible to obtain cabinets except on those rare occasions when second-hand cases came up at auction. Now, however, the manufacture of coin cabinets has become a commercial proposition and an excellent range are produced to suit all tastes and pockets by H. S. Swann of Heddon-on-the-Wall.

Another, though perhaps a minor, disadvantage of the coin cabinet is the inflexibility of the trays, which are pierced with holes of a size which must be just right for the coins which fill them. Trays containing holes large enough to contain sixpences will obviously not admit shillings, while pennies placed in a tray designed for crowns or thalers would look rather lost— unless they happened to be 'cartwheels'. The holes in these trays are usually lined with felt and the coins rest snugly on this, so that only one side may be seen at any time. These dis- advantages, inflexibility and the fact that only one side of the coins is visible, disappear if the collector adopts one of the many types of coin album which are now being marketed in Britain and the United States.

They come in several types, best known of which is probably that manufactured by Whitman of Racine, Wisconsin. Whitman pioneered the coin folder many years ago. Basically this consists of a stout card base with holes tailored to take certain denomina- tions. The card is suitably annotated with such data as date, mint-mark and die, and undoubtedly the appearance of these

attractive folders did much to stimulate type collecting in the
United States, particularly of such coins as the Indian Head and
Lincoln cents. In the past few years Whitman have begun
producing special folders for British and foreign coins other
than the American series and these have become exceedingly
popular here and on the Continent. Whitman folders cover all
denominations from the farthing upwards and embrace the
modern coinage period, so that a complete range of these
folders would be quite sufficient for the majority of modern
British or American collectors.

More recently, however, collectors have begun to favour the
use of special albums consisting of stout acetate pages held in a
ring binder. The pages are fitted with pockets of varying sizes
designed to hold coins from the diminutive third-farthing to the
crown and cartwheel twopence. The best of the British albums
are those produced by Spink's and Philatelic Publishers Ltd.
The latter firm, which has established a wide reputation for the
quality of its albums, manufactures what is probably the best
coin album on the market today. A slight disadvantage of most
coin albums is the fact that the pockets into which the coins are
inserted are open at the top; consequently coins may be dis-
lodged if the album pages are turned hurriedly or carelessly, and
they may sustain irremediable damage as they fall out. The
'Collecta' coin album manufactured by Philatelic Publishers
has a safety device which prevents coins from working loose and
falling out of their pockets.

Coin albums are ideal for two main reasons. The transparent
PVC or acetate pages enable both sides of a coin to be seen
without the necessity of handling the coin at all. The second
advantage is their compactness: an album containing 300 or
more coins takes up an inch of shelving in a bookcase and a
large collection, which would otherwise require several cabinets,
can be housed on one shelf. Coin albums are also relatively
cheap—the most expensive album on the market today is less
than a tenth of the cost of the cheapest cabinet.

The other traditional method of housing a collection—in
small envelopes arranged in vertical rows in narrow boxes—is
now being eclipsed by the coin album. Cheaper and more

compact than the coin cabinet, this method is far less convenient than the album. Until recently the envelopes used were a special manilla with a low moisture content, but nowadays PVC envelopes are increasingly popular. With the former one could write the relevant details concerning a coin on its envelope. The modern plastic envelopes often have a narrow pocket at the top allowing the insertion of a strip of paper or card bearing the necessary data.

Medals, being usually bigger and thicker than coins, are often more difficult to house satisfactorily. Where they are not too large, the coin album or cabinet should suffice, but with the very large pieces a good method is to house them in old cutlery boxes which can be stored in drawers. Cabinets with shallow drawers, such as lepidopterists favour for moths and butterflies, are ideal for a collection of war medals and decorations.

It is important that coins and medals be stored in an even temperature and humidity. The effects of a severe drop in temperature in respect of an unstable metal like tin have already been noted, but while other metals are not so dramatically affected it is advisable that a constant temperature (70°F —21°C, or average room temperature, is adequate) be maintained and, ideally, a humidity of 50%. Fortunately both ideals of temperature and humidity are easy to obtain in the temperate climate of Britain and north-western Europe, while air-conditioning is an increasingly common feature of houses in America.

SELLING COINS AND MEDALS

Many collectors over-value their coins and medals. Consequently, when they eventually come to sell their collections, they are rapidly disillusioned and think that dealers are trying to cheat them. Unfortunately the mushroom growth of numismatics in Britain has given rise to a 'fringe' of unscrupulous individuals who take advantage of the collector by buying cheap and selling dear. This state of affairs is inevitable in the raw state of numismatics today, but, as the hobby matures and collectors become not only more knowledgeable but also more sophisticated, the opportunities for sharp practice in some sections of the trade will gradually die out. I cannot re-iterate too often the necessity of buying from a reputable dealer; the same advice holds good when it comes to selling. In both cases membership of the P.N.A. is a reliable guide to the collector.

Advertisements in the lay press, with offers to buy coins, should be treated with caution. Within recent months, *Coins, Medals and Currency* has exposed the nefarious tactics of certain individuals who have been advertising in the Personal Columns of various newspapers offering absurdly low prices for good quality material. Whereas no serious numismatist is likely to be attracted by such advertisements there may be many readers of these newspapers who just happen to have cased sets, proofs, or Maundy money and who might be duped into parting with them for a fraction of their true worth. This activity has naturally incensed the *bona fide* coin trade who feel that such practices can damage the reputation of the London numismatic market.

Coins, Medals and Currency followed up a typical advertisement which appeared in the Personal Column of *The Times* on 7th January, 1968. It began with the words '£25 paid for 1927 and 1938 coin sets in red cases . . .' These and other offers in this advertisement are listed below, with the contemporary retail selling prices in parentheses:

> 1927 set—£25 (£65–£75); 1937 set—£25 (£45); 1950 set— £12 (£24); 1951 set—£12 (£35–£40); 1953 plastic set— £2 15s. (£10); all George V crowns (except 1935)—£11 each (£32 in commoner years, but £250 for 1934 and £130 for 1936); Victorian or Edwardian Maundy sets—£6 (£12 for commonest set); George VI Maundy set—£8 (£20); Elizabethan Maundy set—£10 (average £30, but Coronation set £75).

An analysis of these prices shows a certain amount of inconsistency. Where the buying price was about half the retail selling price the offer is not all that unreasonable, although marginally lower than the offer which a reputable dealer would make. But a degree of ambiguity or vagueness in the above advertisement could mislead the owner of some of the more choice George V crowns into parting with them for a fraction of their true value. Coin collectors are more fortunate than their confrères who collect fine art or antiques, in that there is no dearth of accurate, up-to-date catalogues and price lists by which a comparison of market values can be easily made. Unfortunately the person who is likely to read such advertisements and be taken in by them is seldom in a position to check these prices through being unaware of the existence of catalogues where some inkling of a coin's value can be ascertained.

There have also been reports of some unscrupulous dealers playing on the fears of honest, law-abiding citizens by persuading them that it is an offence to possess *any* post-1837 gold coins and thereby forcing them to sell them at ridiculously low prices. Fortunately such cases seem to be comparatively rare.

While there is no denying that there is a certain fringe of operators who part collectors from their coins at prices below the market value, the great majority of dealers are honourable men and women with a reputation to protect. On the other hand it all too often happens that collectors over-estimate the worth of their coins, the commonest cause of this being an inability to assess condition accurately. If this book does nothing more than drive home the fact that condition is the most significant factor in deducing the value of a coin I would be doing both collectors and dealers a great service, for it is the condition factor which many collectors fail to grasp properly. Remember that a 1967 half-crown in B. Unc. condition is worth a great deal more *now* than a 1918 KN penny in F condition will ever be—and yet many people, collectors and non-collectors alike, have the fallacy of the supposed value of these pennies deeply engrained in them.

Haphazard accumulations of coins, either schoolboy collections or the dregs of long-forgotten foreign holidays, are sometimes unearthed during spring-cleaning and speculation as to their value begins when the proud possessor borrows a copy of Yeoman from the local library. On this basis even the most jejune accumulations, each coin painstakingly valued according to the price listed in the catalogue, begin to take on a formidable value. On paper, therefore, a collection of 240 coins, all common, base-metal, low denominations priced at a minimum of 10c. each in Yeoman, would be worth £10, but in fact a dealer would be immensely philanthropic if he were to give a fortieth of that sum for them.

In assessing the value of such a collection a dealer will look for the odd item in better-than-average condition, rare dates or mint-marks or unusual pieces; but an accumulation of cheap coins in poor condition is worthless to him. Every dealer inevitably accumulates his own virtually worthless pieces, when he buys mixed lots in order to secure the finer specimens, and he is unlikely to go out of his way, or part with good money, in order to buy worthless items *per se*. I remember the case of an acquaintance of mine who had a tin box full of coins accumulated during a lifetime's residence in India. He eventually decided to sell the coins and took them from one dealer to another but each declined to purchase the collection since it contained no outstanding items and its condition was poor. Eventually he took his coins to a dealer who refused to buy the coins, but offered him £2 for the box in which they were housed—an interesting example of a Victorian chocolate box, which had acquired an antiquarian value in its own right!

Haphazard accumulations are seldom valuable unless the person collecting the coins was in a position to acquire good material by being in the right place at the right time. For collections to be worth a lot of money, either a lot of money must have been spent on them or the collector must have selected his specimens with discernment and shrewdly profited from his superior knowledge to spot the bargains when they have been going and to realise the significance of material which was of no account to everybody else. Such collections, built up carefully, using only the finest specimens available, tastefully arranged in albums or cabinets and written up to show the numismatist's knowledge to best advantage, are the ones which make a profit and find a ready market.

If you have collected wisely and built up a good collection you should not experience much difficulty in disposing of it when the time comes. Of course, it is good policy to have some

idea of its value before trying to sell it and this can be estimated
in several ways. Some collectors keep a detailed account of their
purchases so that, at any time, they can tell how much money
they have spent on the collection. This in itself is a useful basis
to work on. Depending on the type and quality of the collection
and the length of time which has elapsed since the material was
bought, the collector can gauge realistically the worth of his
coins and medals.

For other numismatists a more rough-and-ready method is
the answer. On the supposition that, were the collection to be
offered intact to a dealer, the coins of low value will be dis-
counted, it is a good rule to reckon up the value of the better
items alone—say those whose catalogue price is 5s. or $1 or more.
Even then the total sum would have to be divided by two or
three to arrive at a true market value—unless the collection
were a particularly fine one, containing coins at present in great
demand, in which case the offering price might be closer to the
catalogue figure.

As in purchasing coins and medals there are several ways of
selling them: to a dealer, to another collector, by private
treaty, by auction, and by splitting them up and selling them
piecemeal by advertising in the numismatic magazines or
through the local numismatic society. The best method, for a
quick sale yet getting a good price, is to sell to another collector.
In this way there are no dealers' profits or auctioneers' commission to be considered.

The other quick way of cashing a collection, though not
usually so profitable, is selling it to a dealer. He may well have a
customer waiting for just such a collection as yours (particularly
if he deals in a fairly specialised type of material) and thus his
turnover will be quick. Or he may pick out the gems to sell to
his better clients and then break up the remainder, putting the
individual sets and odd items into his general stock.

Selling through an auctioneer is a much slower process. It
may take several months for a collection to be lotted (i.e.
broken up into lots of suitable size) and described, so that the
descriptions given in the sale catalogue will be as accurate as
possible. Since the auctioneer gets his commission from the

vendor it is in his own interest to see that nothing of value or significance is overlooked in the description of lots. Then the sales catalogues have to be printed and mailed to the auctioneer's regular clients (often numbering several thousands) several weeks before the sale so that they will have ample time to study them. Payment is usually made within a short time after the sale has taken place. The auctioneer forwards a list of the lot numbers with the sum realised for each one noted against them. From the total figure is deduced the auctioneer's commission plus any other charges incurred. The latter may include photographic fees. Since the vendor may need to sell his collection in a hurry in order to raise money quickly the time lag in auctioning material may be a deterrent; but some auctioneers are prepared these days to make a cash advance, based on a proportion of their valuation of a collection. Such an advance is, of course, subject to the usual interest but this is normally deducted from the net sum realised (i.e. after deduction of commission).

Another method of sale undertaken by some dealers and auctioneers is by private treaty. In this way collections are offered intact, through the medium of advertisements, direct to other collectors. This method offers a saving in both time and money to all parties concerned and allows the vendor to salve his conscience at parting with his collection by knowing that it is going intact to a good home. This method of disposing of coins and medals is, surprisingly, little used in spite of the many points to commend it. Thus collections which have taken a lifetime to build up, seldom survive as an entity once they have been entrusted to a dealer or auctioneer to sell.

Advertising material for sale direct to other collectors is a satisfactory method of disposing of it, providing that you are not in a great hurry for results. All the commercial numismatic periodicals carry classified advertisements inserted by collectors. The rates for these advertisements are very reasonable but, since most magazines appear only monthly, anything up to three months may elapse between placing the advertisement and seeing it in print. Provided you stick to accurate descriptions and your prices are competitive you should not experience much difficulty in selling coins and medals in this way. An interesting feature of *Coins, Medals and Currency* is the weekly Coin Tray which consists of circles containing photographs of items which both collectors and dealers have for disposal. The charges for each circle and photographic reproduction are very moderate and there is no doubt that a good quality picture (produced, in this case, by the web offset process) gives a great boost to selling. In cases like this, however, the initial outlay is only worthwhile if you have more than one example of a particular coin for sale, or if the value of the coin is relatively great. It is also worthwhile scanning the dealers' advertisements since they often contain details of the material which they wish to purchase, together with the prices paid.

CHAPTER XII

LEGAL AND FISCAL ASPECTS OF NUMISMATICS

Like any other form of property, a valuable collection of coins and medals has its legal and tax problems. If you own some property it is in your own best interests to look after it. In recent years there has been an alarming increase in the number of coin thefts and burglaries in Britain and America. In recent months robberies have ranged from military medals taken from Southsea Castle to a suitcase in Camden Town containing three coin albums. Not so long ago Seaby's entire stock of gold coins was stolen and, more recently, a valuable collection of Anglo-Saxon pennies vanished. Scarcely a week passes without a crime of this sort being reported in the national as well as the numismatic press. There is little remedy, but museums and exhibitions are tightening up their security, while it behoves the private collector and the individual dealer to ensure that he is insured.

Normally, those companies with whom you have your household contents insured will also extend cover to coin collections, provided that the value of the latter in proportion to the other goods and chattels is not above a certain percentage. The practice in this matter varies from one company to another, so it is necessary to clear up this point at the outset. Where a collection of coins and medals is coverable by the normal household policy there is usually a limit on the value of any single item. If you have a few coins which each exceed 10% of the value of the collection as a whole it will usually be necessary to get a special numismatic insurance policy to cover these items adequately. Many of the larger dealers and auctioneers also act as valuers and insurance brokers, so it is worth while to consult them for precise details in each case.

The insurance company may require an independent valuation set on your collection (particularly if it is a large and valuable one) and will appoint one of their accredited experts to carry out the assessment. The cost of these valuations is calculated either on the time involved or, more usually, as a percentage of the final value. Valuations and insurance premiums are not cheap but, with coin thefts on the increase, no collector can afford to do without some safeguard against loss. Money may be small compensation for the loss of a collection which has taken a lifetime to build up and which contains many irreplaceable items, but it is better than nothing at all and with the insurance collected one can always start all over again.

If your collection is a more modest one the insurance company may accept your own valuation. In arriving at this figure you should remember that it is the replacement value of the collection which is required. On the one hand a valuation based on Yeoman's or Seaby's full catalogue prices would be regarded as unrealistic; on the other hand some collectors tend to forget that numismatic values are rising inevitably as the value of money falls (particularly since the devaluation of sterling in November 1967) and thus they neglect to keep their valuations up to date. It would be rather tedious to revalue a collection every year but the value should be reviewed every five years at least.

For this purpose a little book work is necessary. Some form of inventory should be compiled giving a brief description of the items, sets of covers, with their catalogue numbers and five-yearly valuations. The date and cost of the purchase could also be noted where practicable. This may not be necessary for items of moderate or low value, but, where valuable items are concerned, this is now a vital matter since, under the terms of the 1965 Finance Act, you may be required to disclose to the Commissioners of Inland Revenue the cost of such assets and from whom they were acquired. For this reason, moreover, it is essential to obtain a bill of sale and to keep a file of all receipts where the sum involved is large.

Apart from their usefulness to the insurance company, numismatic inventories are of vital importance to executors.

Many numismatists, extremely efficient in their business or profession, have unfortunately been quite unbusinesslike where their hobby was concerned. Wives seldom know how much money their husbands lavish on their coins. In many cases they have regarded their husband's pastime with amused indulgence, partly condescending and partly tolerant, with little realisation of the value or importance of the asset which is being built up.

Few wives ever take a real interest in their husband's hobby and consequently when a collector dies, his widow is often at a loss (a) to appreciate the value of the collection and (b) to know what to do with it. If you have spent a lot of money on your coins you owe it to your wife or dependants to make an inventory (a copy of which should be kept with the collection) and written instructions regarding the eventual disposal of the collection. If possible, a numismatic executor should be appointed. In the 'big league' those dealers, who have given a great deal of time to building up a collection for a client, often act as numismatic executors; but usually some close friend who shares the hobby will suffice.

If the collection is to be sold or auctioned off after the death of the owner written instructions to that effect should be left with the numismatic executor and, if possible, a dealer or auctioneer nominated to handle the negotiations. The disposal of a collection has many advantages, particularly when it is considered in relation to the rest of the estate.

In the United Kingdom estate duty has to be paid on all estates totalling more than £5,000—and this sum can easily be reached by the most modest estate providing the testator owns a house, car, furnishings, etc. The wealthier you are the greater will be the percentage of duty to which your estate is liable and a coin collection can be a useful asset to realise in order to settle the estate duty without having to disturb commercial investments and other property. A coin collection is usually of great *personal* interest only to the collector himself and it will often be less of a wrench for his widow to dispose of it than it might be if she were forced to liquidate share holdings or sell her house to meet the estate duty.

The majority of the collectors personally known to me are in the lower range of the wealth scale and few of them have any commercial investments worth talking about. Such surplus cash as they have tends to be invested in their coin collections. In some cases—and these are by no means isolated—there are numismatists who adopt an almost miserly approach to everything except their coin collection. Coin collecting is an addiction to them.

You may not wish to have your collection sold off after your death. You may not agree with the views of Edmond de Goncourt, who stated in his will, 'My wish is that my drawings, my prints, my curiosities, my books—those objects of art which have been the job of my life—shall not be consigned to the cold tomb of a museum, and so laid out to the foolish glancing of the careless passer-by; but I will that all shall be dispersed by the hammer of the auctioneers, so that the pleasure which the acquiring of each one of these has given me shall be given once again, in every case, to someone, the inheritor of my own tastes.'

It is possible that, after a lifetime's investment and study, you have put together an incomparable collection which has won you a reputation among your fellow numismatists. Having shrewdly collected the coins or medals of your particular field, perhaps when it was unfashionable, you have now assembled a collection which could never be formed again, and were it to be dispersed in the sale-room something which you have created would be lost for ever. How can you ensure that your collection lives on after you, in a way immortalising you? The obvious answer is to present it to some museum, with a deed of donation drawn up to ensure that the collection is to be maintained intact and not broken up, merged with any other collections, sold or otherwise dispersed. Pressure of space and shortage of money prevent museums from being able to put all their collections (numismatic or otherwise) on permanent exhibition —even if this were desirable, which is questionable since such a display often hinders the research student from close and detailed examination of the material.

Bequests to museums or other national institutions may be facilitated by certain concessions in the estate duty law of most countries. Under Section 40 of the Finance Act of 1930 (United

Kingdom), for example, objects or collections which are deemed to be of historic, national, artistic or scientific interest may be exempted from death duties. This is a reasonable concession to those who possess a priceless Leonardo, a Caxton incunable or a Fabergé Easter Egg, things which are in the nature of heirlooms handed down from generation to generation. No tax is paid on such items, which are considered as worthy of inclusion in the appropriate national collection, provided that they are not sold.

The only instance where you can 'eat your cake and still have it' in this respect is if the object or collection is sold to the British Museum. If circumstances make it necessary for you to part with the family heirlooms this is one way of avoiding the payment of estate duty, an inducement for you not to dispose of priceless treasures to the detriment of the national heritage.

The exemption of coins under Section 40 of the Finance Act, 1930, does not mean that you have to surrender them to the 'appropriate national collection'. Putting it bluntly, investment in coins of the highest quality, such as to merit exemption, is a shrewd way of passing on to your heirs a form of property without having it whittled away by estate duty. This is an asset which does not earn you or your heirs a regular income, in the way that commercial investments would, but is an asset which withstands the fall in value of money and should appreciate *per se* as the years go by.

Applications for exemption can only be made after decease; there is no way of arranging this before-hand and you are not permitted to die safe in the knowledge that your heirs and successors will not be forced to sell the collection to pay the death duty on it. You can, however, leave clear instructions to your solicitors and your numismatic executor telling them to apply for exemption. If this were more widely realised a number of fine collections would still be in existence today as potential national assets instead of having been dispersed (often abroad) to pay taxes which could, and ought to, have been avoided.

The situation in the United States is a great deal more liberal. Estate duty, introduced in 1916, has always been more leniently levied and has never had the crippling effect which is sometimes felt in Britain. Moreover, generous tax concessions are given to collectors during their lifetime, enabling them to plough back tax gains into their hobby (whether it be stamps, coins, ceramics or paintings) if they are earmarked for national collections. In this way, for example, the bequests to the Smithsonian Institution in Washington have been enormous in scope and value in recent years.

At the time of writing, special legislation is being drafted in the United States Congress in an effort to save a very valuable collection for the nation. The millionaire industrialist, Josiah K. Lilly, who died in May 1966, formed a collection comprising more than 6,000 rare gold coins valued at the time of his death at $5½ millions (£1,977,000 before devaluation). Ironically he died ten hours before he was due to see his lawyer with the intention, it is believed, of adding a codicil to his will leaving his coins to the Smithsonian. Now a special tax law is necessary to grant the estate relief from duty on the collection which would otherwise have to be broken up in the process.

Since the passage of the Finance Act 1965, British collectors have been faced with capital gains tax. Broadly speaking, this tax is payable on capital gains (profit) made on transactions involving the buying and selling of stocks and shares, land and property. No tax is liable, however, on any profit made on the sale of one's private residence (provided it has been owned for at least twelve months) or on profits on the sale of such things as coins, stamps, jewellery, paintings and *objets d'art* provided that the item in question is under £1,000 in value.

This tax came into operation in the financial year 1965–6 (i.e. from the 6th April, 1965) and it is from this date that the value and the resulting profit is to be computed. From that date onwards it has become more than ever necessary for collectors to keep exact records of their collections, with an accurate valuation, supported wherever possible by bills of sale and receipts for each new major purchase.

Even at the time of writing, the position regarding capital gains tax is none too clear and I must qualify my statement by adding that the interpretation of the 1965 Finance Act may be subject to change (and, of course, there is always the possibility that further legislation may also alter the situation).

At present it has been held that the £1,000 criterion affecting the payment of tax is to apply not to a collection as a whole but to its components. Thus a collection might fetch £10,000 as a whole, but if it is broken up into a dozen lots of £800–£900 each, no capital gains tax will be liable. If a lot did fetch more than £1,000, tax would be assessed on the difference between the value of the lot at 6th April, 1965, and the sum realised, less the auctioneer's commission and any other incidentals such as valuer's and solicitor's fees.

The standard rate of tax on capital gains is 30%, at present, but the percentage may be considerably less, depending on the vendor's level of income and the rate at which he pays surtax (if any). Surtax *may* be avoided if the net gains from numismatic selling are taxed as income, in cases where the total income is less than £5,000 a year. Taxed separately, surtax might be liable on numismatic earnings if earned income from other sources exceeds £3,000. In problems of this kind it is always advisable to seek the counsel of a good accountant. Furthermore, long-term and short-term gains must be kept separate. Short-term gains are those made on items bought and sold within twelve months, while long-term gains are those made over a longer period.

* * * * *

Finally, there is an important aspect of buying and selling coins and medals which should be discussed. It is important, if possible, to know that the material you are collecting is what it appears to be and not a fake or forgery. With the more expensive items it is virtually necessary these days to establish their pedigree. It is advisable, when spending a lot of money on a coin or a medal, to have it authenticated and, conversely, when disposing of such an item it obviously facilitates the sale if it has a certificate of authenticity or at least the signature of an acknowledged expert.

There is unfortunately no numismatic counterpart of the various philatelic bodies which will expertise stamps and issue certificates guaranteeing their authenticity. The P.N.A.,

I.A.P.N. and other professional numismatic organisations, however, bind their members to guarantee the genuineness of the coins and medals they sell.

TREASURE TROVE

Objects of gold or silver (including coins, plate and bullion) which have been hidden in the ground or in buildings, and of which the original owner cannot be traced, are considered to be 'Treasure Trove'. This concept has grown up in English Common Law, without any clear precedents in Roman or Teutonic law. By the twelfth century it was established as one of the rights of the monarch.

Broadly speaking there are four factors involved. Firstly, the material deposited is important; only gold and silver come into this category and not only coins but ornaments, vessels, or even weapons are involved if these metals are present. Secondly, the method of deposit is significant. The emphasis has invariably been on deliberate concealment, the depositor intending to retrieve it at some later date. In one case, however, the so-called Credit on Treasure Trove of 1896, a coroner's jury deemed that a bag of gold coins found in the wall of a house was Treasure Trove, though the circumstances seem to indicate accidental rather than deliberate concealment. The coins, with some papers and a tobacco pipe, were found lying on a beam which had obviously served as a shelf in an office, and during alterations had inadvertently been plastered over.

Thirdly, the place of deposit must be considered. Formerly this was defined as 'hidden in the ground' and arose from the age-old right of the king to treasure in graves and burial mounds. In recent cases, however, hoards concealed above ground have been adjudged Treasure Trove. Such instances include holes in the walls or in the roofs of buildings. Fourthly, it must be proved that the original owner or his heirs cannot be traced—a straightforward matter in the majority of cases.

If you find any coins the police should be notified. A coroner's inquest is convened under the Coroners Act 1887, section 36 and experts (usually staff of the British Museum) are called to give evidence on the nature of the find and enable the coroner to decide whether the material constitutes Treasure Trove. If it is so adjudged it automatically becomes the property of the Crown, unless, as in some cases, the 'Franchise of Treasure Trove' has been expressly granted to a subject in so far as finds of a particular locality are concerned, such as the County Palatine of Lancaster and the Duchy of Cornwall. Treasure Trove found in the City of London belongs to the Corporation and invariably ends up in the Guildhall Museum.

In England the Crown may decide to sell the coins to a museum, normally the British Museum, or in some cases, one or other of the great national museums, or even the museum of the locality where the find was made. The finder is seldom permitted to keep his finds, which may seem harsh. In the Middle Ages punishment for concealing Treasure Trove from the proper authorities was death or mutilation, but since 1348 it has been classed as a misdemeanour punishable by a fine or imprisonment. Conversely finders of Treasure Trove are always compensated with a reward—tax free—equal to the present market value of the coins. If the coins are not required for a museum, they are returned to the finder to dispose of as he will. If he so desires, the British Museum will arrange to sell them for him at the best price obtainable.

The present system of giving the British Museum first pick arose in the mid-eighteenth century when the Museum was founded, at the same time as the hereditary rights and revenues of the Crown (which included Treasure Trove) were surrendered in return for the fixed annual income known as the Civil List.

In Scotland the same general procedure applies, except that the Queen's Remembrancer and Treasurer for Scotland acts as the recipient of all finds and first choice of rare coins is given to the Royal Scottish Museum in Edinburgh.

If the coroner decides that more than one person was concerned in the finding, then the reward may be divided; but it should be emphasised that the reward is made to the actual finder or finders and not to the owner or occupier of the land.

INDEX